THE LAW OF FLORIDA HOMEOWNERS ASSOCIATIONS

Single Family Subdivisions
Townhouse & Cluster Developments
Master Community Associations

10th Edition

Peter M. Dunbar, Esq.
and Charles F. Dudley, Esq.

Pineapple Press, Inc.
Sarasota, Florida

Copyright © 2014 by Peter M. Dunbar and Charles F. Dudley

All rights reserved. No part of this book may be reproduced in any form or by any means, electronic or mechanical, including photocopying, recording, or by any information storage and retrieval system, without permission in writing from the publisher.

Note: Chapter 10, Association Forms and Documents, may be reproduced without publisher's permission.

Inquiries should be addressed to:
Pineapple Press, Inc.
P.O. Box 3889
Sarasota, Florida 34230

www.pineapplepress.com

ISBN 978-1-56164-722-4

Tenth Edition
Pb 10 9 8 7 6 5 4 3 2 1

Printed in the United States of America

About the Authors

Peter M. Dunbar is the managing officer of the Tallahassee office of the Dean Mead law firm. For almost three years before returning to private practice, he served in the Office of the Governor of the State of Florida as general counsel and later as chief of staff. Before joining Governor Martinez's staff, he was in private practice and specialized in the areas of real property and community association law. Mr. Dunbar is an adjunct professor at Florida State University College of Law and has taught and lectured on associations and the laws governing community living since 1974. He is a member of the Florida Bar and the American College of Real Estate Lawyers, and he graduated with honors from the College of Law at Florida State University.

Mr. Dunbar served as a member of the Florida House of Representatives for ten years. During his legislative career, he served as a member of the House Judiciary Committee and sponsored or co-sponsored every major new law affecting community associations.

Charles F. Dudley is an attorney in private practice in Tallahassee, Florida. In his professional capacity, he is involved on a daily basis with policy makers and administrators in both the legislative and executive branches of Florida's state government. In recent legislative sessions, Mr. Dudley has contributed to the development of the changes in Florida's housing laws for condominiums, cooperatives, mobile homes, and homeowners associations. Mr. Dudley also serves as general counsel to the Florida Cable Telecommunications Association and served as a member of the 1996 Florida Telecommunications Taxation Task Force.

An honors graduate of the College of Law at Florida State University, Mr. Dudley is a member of the Florida Bar. He has been a guest columnist on the law of homeowners associations for *Community Living* and other publications, and he continues to be involved in the pending changes to Florida's housing laws. Mr. Dudley was featured as one of Florida's "Next Wave" of leaders in the December 1993 issue of *Florida Trend* magazine.

Contents

6 RIGHTS AND RESPONSIBILITIES OF THE PARCEL OWNER

7 COVENANTS AND USE OF ASSOCIATION PROPERTY

8 ARCHITECTURAL CONTROL AND STANDARDS

9 RIGHTS AND RESPONSIBILITIES

10 STYLE AND FORMAT FOR ASSOCIATION FORMS AND DOCUMENTS

Introduction

In 1992, special laws governing homeowners associations in Florida were enacted for the first time. In 1995 and in subsequent years, the special statutory provisions were expanded and refined. Prior to these enactments, the general corporate law of Florida governed the affairs of the corporate associations. In 2000, the special statutory provisions relating to mandatory homeowners associations were assigned to a separate chapter of the Florida Statutes—Chapter 720. Today, the general corporate law and the special homeowners associations provisions harmonize to provide the framework for association operation. This manual is offered as a guide to assist those who are governed by a homeowners association in Florida.

The residents who assume positions of responsibility as officers and directors of homeowners associations will be the key to its success or the catalyst for its failure. The association is created to preserve the concept of planned residential living, and the officers and directors are charged with the responsibility of insuring its success. These responsibilities can be significant and their implementation is governed by formal procedures that may be both new and confusing to community leaders.

Leaders of the homeowners associations are, in almost all cases, volunteers and residents of the community. They are confronted with enforcing the covenants and restrictions among their neighbors and balancing community goals and the rights of individual owners.

The officers and directors carry out their duties within the formal confines of the governing documents, the rules of parliamentary procedure, and applicable law. Collectively, these formal standards assure fairness and uniformity for community residents and present a unique challenge to the community leaders. The formalities prescribe notice and require open meetings. They establish eligibility and set standards of conduct for officers and directors, and they provide the methods by which the membership may express its collective will.

Formal policies and procedures do not have to be unnecessarily complicated and they should not frustrate the substantive goals of the homeowners association. This manual is designed as a practical guide to assist community leaders with their duties and responsibilities, and as a reference tool to assure the successful operation of the homeowners association.

This manual provides a step-by-step explanation of the statutory requirements for meetings, membership voting and the parliamentary procedures that govern gatherings of the association and its board of directors. It contains sets of forms and sample documents for use by community leaders, and seeks to provide answers to the basic questions that arise from time to time on the operation of the community.

When officers and directors approach implementation of their duties, the authors hope that this manual will assist them and their advisors with problems of procedure and association organization. It is offered to simplify and clarify the formal and technical elements of association operation. By doing so, the main role of the homeowners association can be successfully carried out and the organization will function correctly for the benefit of its member-residents.

1

The Homeowners Association and the Community Concept

1.1 Homeowners Association Concept. Mandatory homeowners associations are the cornerstones for many of Florida's planned residential communities. Properly run, they promote the community concept and protect the community's property values. Under Florida's state and local land development regulations governing residential properties, homeowners associations are often assigned significant responsibilities to provide services and to maintain improvements within the community such as roadways and drainage structures.[1] In many cases, homeowners associations also make available recreational and other facilities that might not otherwise be affordable or available to homeowners and residents.

Historically, homeowners associations have been organized under the Florida Not For Profit Corporation Act (Chapter 617 of the Florida Statutes) and have operated under the general provisions of corporate law.[2] Although efforts to provide special statutory provisions to govern the operations of mandatory homeowners associations had been attempted for years, it was not until 1992 that these efforts were successful.[3] In 1995 and in subsequent years, the Legislature expanded the special statutory provisions for the operation of most of Florida's traditional mandatory homeowners associations.[4] In 2000, these special provisions were reassigned to Chapter 720 of the Florida Statutes.[5]

Associations subject to regulation by Chapter 718 (Condominium Act), Chapter 719 (Cooperative Act), Chapter 721 (Florida Vacation Plan and Time-Sharing Act), and Chapter 723 (Florida Mobile Home Act) are not governed by the special homeowners association provisions in Chapter 720 of the Florida Statutes. Associations governing communities that are comprised of property primarily intended for commercial, industrial, or other non-residential use are also exempt from the special provisions in the law governing mandatory homeowners associations.[6]

For all other homeowners associations responsible for the operation of a community where membership is a mandatory condition for the owners of property upon which assessments are required and may become a lien on the parcel, the homeowners association provisions of Chapter 720 of the Florida Statutes apply.[7] The statutory scheme of Chapter 720 is

---

1   §720.302 (1), F.S.
2   §617.002, F.S.
3   The Residential Planned Development Study Commission, "Report to the Florida Legislature," at 1 (Jan. 24, 1985) (on file at the Florida Legislative Library).
4   Chapter 720, *Florida Statutes.*
5   Chapter 2000-258, *Laws of Florida.*
6   §720.302 (3), F.S.
7   §720.301 (8) and (11), F.S.

comprehensive and a county or city may not enact an ordinance imposing additional or more stringent requirements for homeowners associations.[8]

1.2   Applicable Law and Legislative Intent. While other parts of the corporate law found in Chapter 617 of the Florida Statutes affect mandatory homeowners associations in Florida, Chapter 720 of the Florida Statutes gives special recognition to those corporations that operate residential communities in the state. These designated sections of Chapter 720 set out specific operational procedures for homeowners associations while providing for the protection of individual rights of association members.[9]

In its enactment of these special sections of the law in 1995, the Legislature also made a series of basic findings concerning the law of Florida homeowners associations. First, the law is intended to protect the rights of property owners and association members without unduly impairing the association's ability to perform its functions. Next, the contract rights created for the benefit of the association and its members in the declaration of covenants governing the community are not to be impaired by the law. And finally, the Legislature determined that it was not in the best interests of either the homeowners association or its members to create an agency of government to regulate association affairs.[10]

1.3   The Community. The "community" under Chapter 720 of the Florida Statutes includes all of the real property that is, or will be, subject to the declaration of covenants governing the property. Included in the statutory definition of "community" are not only the common areas owned or leased by the association but also those lands and leaseholds that are subject to the jurisdiction of the homeowners association including the lots, parcels, or tracts of individual owners.[11]

A "parcel," lot, or tract is the real property within the community that is subject to separate conveyance and exclusive ownership. The parcel may be either platted or unplatted and its owner, or an association in which the owner is a member, must be required to pay homeowners association assessments that, if not paid, may result in a lien against the parcel.[12]

Common areas and recreational facilities serving a homeowners association and its members are also included within the definition of the community. The common areas may be owned or leased by the

---

8   *Advisory Opinion of the Florida Attorney General, AGO 2001-01.*
9   §720.302 (1), F.S.
10   §720.302 (1) and (2), F.S.
11   §720.301 (3), F.S.
12   §720.301 (11), F.S.

association, or they may be dedicated to the association or its members by recorded plat.[13] Regardless of how the common areas are owned, ad valorem taxes and special assessments may not be assessed separately against the common areas used by the parcel owners in the subdivision.[14] These common areas include all of the property not included within the boundaries of the individual lots, including recreational parcels, easement areas for the benefit of the subdivision, and areas such as drainage retention ponds designated on the plat or site plan.[15]

The common areas serving the community must be made available to parcel owners and their invited guests to use as the property was intended.[16] A parcel owner's right to assemble in the common areas or in the facilities cannot be unreasonably restricted, and an owner may enforce his or her right to use the common area through mediation and in court.[17] (See 6.2.) The right of an owner to use the common areas may be denied for a reasonable time, however, when an owner has failed to comply with the community covenants or when the owner is delinquent in the assessment obligation to the association.[18] (See 5.10 and 6.2.) The association also has a responsibility to protect those who use and occupy the common areas of the community from foreseeable hazards.[19]

1.4 The Homeowners Association. The corporate entity responsible for the operation of the community created by the declaration of covenants is known as the "homeowners association," or simply as the "association."[20] In Florida, it is permissible, and not uncommon, to find that the homeowners association operates more than one community.[21] The association must be a Florida corporation and its voting membership must be made up of the parcel owners in the community or their designated agents.[22] It is permissible for the homeowners association to have more than one class of members.[23]

---

13   §720.301 (2), F.S.; see also §177.081, F.S.
14   §193.0235 (1), F.S.
15   §193.0235 (2), F.S.
16   *Blue Reef Holding Corp., Inc. v. Coyne, 545 So.2d 1053 (Fla. 4th DCA 1994); Lewis v. S & T Anchorage, Inc., 616 So.2d 478 (Fla. 3d DCA 1993).*
17   §720.304 (1), F.S.
18   §720.305 (2) (b), F.S.
19   *Barrwood Homeowners Ass'n, Inc. v. Maser, 675 So.2d 983 (Fla. 4th DCA 1996); Sanzare v. Varesi, 681 So.2d 785 (Fla. 4th DCA 1996).*
20   §720.301 (7), F.S. The term "homeowners association" does not include a community development district or other special taxing district created pursuant to statute. Homeowners association members may, however, be subject to a special taxing district. See *Chambless v. The Officers and Directors of Snapper Creek, 743 So.2d 129 (Fla. 3d DCA 1999).*
21   §720.302 (1), F.S.; see also *Homeowner's Ass'n of Overlook, Inc. v. Seabrooke Homeowner's Ass'n, Inc., 62 So.3d 667 (Fla. 4th DCA 2011).*
22   §720.301 (8), F.S. and §720.302 (5), F.S.
23   §720.303 (1), F.S.

Membership in the association is a mandatory condition of parcel ownership in the community, and the association is authorized to impose assessments against its members that, if unpaid, may become a lien against the parcel owned by the member.[24] Each homeowners association is authorized by statute to enforce the covenants and restrictions contained in the governing documents of the community[25] and the law also permits the association to suspend the rights of a parcel owner to use the common areas of the community for a violation of the restrictions in the governing documents.[26] (See 7.5.)

1.5 Assessments. To fund the operations, amenities, and special needs of a homeowners association, each parcel owner is required to contribute a proportionate share of the costs and expenses.[27] Each owner's proportionate share of the annual budget and the general operations and obligations of the association is referred to in statute as an "assessment" or an "amenity fee." The assessments or amenity fees may be payable to the association, to the developer, or to another owner of property serving the community. Under the statutes and the documents governing the community, any fees or assessments remaining unpaid by a parcel owner may become a lien on the parcel until the assessment is paid.[28] (See 5.9.)

The purposes for which a homeowners association may levy a charge or an assessment against a parcel must be identified in the articles of incorporation, bylaws, or other documents governing the community.[29] The homeowners association is required to maintain a current account and a periodic statement of the account for each member of the association. The account must designate the member's name, the due date and amount of each assessment, the amount paid upon the account, and the balance due.[30]

---

24 §720.301 (1) and (8), F.S.; see also *Rosenberg v. Metrowest Master Ass'n, Inc., 116 So3d 641 (Fla. 5th DCA 2013).*

25 §720.303 (1), F.S.; Rule 1.221, Florida Rules of Civil Procedure.

26 §720.305 (1) and (2), F.S. Pursuant to §810.09 (3), the association may also be designated as an "authorized person" to enforce trespass violations on a construction site.

27 §720.308 (1); see also *Wood v. McElvey, 296 So.2d 102 (Fla. 2d DCA 1974).*

28 §720.301 (1), F.S.; see also *Bennett v. Behring Corp., 466 F. Supp. 689 (S.D. Fla. 1979) holding that the constitutional protection of homestead does not necessarily invalidate a debt or lien but may under certain circumstances take priority.*

29 *Wenger v. Breakwater Homeowners' Ass'n, 423 So.2d 619, 621 (Fla. 4th DCA 1982), citing Orlando Orange Grove Co. v. Hale, 107 Fla. 304, 311, 144 So. 674, 676 (1932) holding a corporation may only exercise those powers conferred by the articles of incorporation or those powers necessary to carry out authorized functions.*

30 §720.303 (4) (j) 2., F.S.

1.6   Declaration of Covenants.

A covenant is a commitment, agreement, or contract which grants a right or imposes a liability.[31] The recorded documents in each community include many such rights, liabilities, and commitments governing the use and occupancy of the property governed by the homeowners association. The documents containing these rights, liabilities, and commitments, i.e., the restrictive covenants or deed restrictions, are defined in Chapter 720 of the Florida Statutes as the "declaration of covenants" or "declaration" for the community.[32]

The recorded declaration of covenants for the community "runs with the land" as a set of permanent restrictions governing its use. The restrictions are equitable rights arising out of the contractual relationship between and among the parcel owners in the community.[33] The restrictions and covenants subject the community to the jurisdiction and control of the homeowners association, and they remain effective until the covenants and restrictions are terminated or until they are found to be no longer necessary.[34] While the declaration of covenants is in effect, the provisions are enforceable by and against each parcel owner.[35] (See 7.4 and 7.5.)

When covenants run with the land, a person who assumes ownership of a parcel of the land also assumes ownership with the presumed knowledge of the covenants.[36] In other words, each new parcel owner is presumed to know and understand the content of the documents governing the homeowners association and the community. It is the responsibility of the original developer to supply copies of the governing documents to initial purchasers, and it is the seller's responsibility to do so if the sale is by an owner who is not the developer. These disclosures must be made prior to the execution of a contract for sale.[37] (See 6.8.)

The recorded declaration of covenants for the community may include the articles of incorporation and bylaws for the homeowners association or the declaration may incorporate them as exhibits. The

---

31   *Black's Law Dictionary, 5th Ed. Rev.; see generally Venetian Isles Homeowners Assoc., Inc. v. Albrecht, 823 So.2d 813 (Fla. 2d DCA 2002); Regency Highland Associates v. Sherwood, 388 So.2d 271 (Fla. 4th DCA 1980), rev. den., 397 So.2d 778 and Balzer v. Indian Lake Maintenance, Inc., 346 So.2d 146 (Fla. 2d DCA 1977).*

32   §720.301 (4), F.S.; see also *Voight v. Harbour Heights Improvement Ass'n, 218 So.2d 803, 806 (Fla. 4th DCA 1969).*

33   *Cudjoe Gardens Property Owners Assoc., Inc. v. Payne, 779 So.2d 598 (Fla. 3d DCA 2001).*

34   §720.301 (4), F.S.; see also *Crissman v. Dedakis, 330 So.2d 103 (Fla. 1st DCA 1976); Bartow v. Moline Properties, 121 Fla. 683, 164 So.551 (Fla. 1935) holding that when covenants lack expressed expiration, a reasonable limitation is implied.*

35   §720.305 (1), F.S.; *see also Loch Haven Homeowners' Ass'n v. Nelle, 389 So.2d 697 (Fla. 2d DCA 1980), affirmed, 413 So.2d 28 (1982).*

36   *Hagan v. Sabal Palms, Inc., 186 So.2d 302, 312–13 (Fla. 2d DCA 1966).*

37   §720.401 (1), F.S.

declaration of covenants together with all duly adopted and recorded amendments and exhibits as well as the articles of incorporation and the bylaws for the association are known as the "governing documents" for the community,[38] and the governing documents are considered a contract between the association and the homeowners bound by the documents.[39] The initial governing documents must be recorded in the official records of the county in which the community is located,[40] and together, the governing documents combine to set out both the powers and the limitations of the homeowners association.[41]

In communities created after October 1, 1998, the law prohibits the inclusion of certain provisions in the governing documents for the community. In the event such provisions do appear in the covenants, the statute declares them to be unenforceable. Among the provisions that are not permitted are (i.) the unilateral right of the developer to make changes to the community's documents after transition; (ii.) limitations or restrictions on the right of the homeowners association to sue the developer; and (iii.) provisions purporting to give weighted voting rights to the developer after transition.[42] Each of these provisions, as well as variations of each, is declared to be null and void as a matter of public policy.[43]

1.7   Articles of Incorporation. The articles of incorporation, or corporate charter, is the document which establishes the homeowners association.[44] The term "articles of incorporation" includes the original document creating the association and all amendments to it and any other documents which define the existing form, membership, and responsibility of the homeowners association. For example, the definition also includes articles of consolidation or articles of merger if several homeowners associations have been combined into a single organization.[45] The articles of incorporation enumerate the powers with which the homeowners association is vested, and its powers are limited to those specifically expressed, and those implied powers necessary to perform the authorized functions of the association.[46]

---

38   §720.301 (6), F.S. See *Highland Lakes Prop. Owners v. Schlack, 724 So.2d 621 (Fla. 5th DCA 1998).*

39   *Thomas v. Vision I Homeowners Ass'n, 981 So.2d 1 (Fla. 4th DCA 2007) and Royal Oak Landing Homeowners Ass'n v. Pelletier, 620 So.2d 786, 788 (Fla. 4th DCA 1993).*

40   §720.303 (1), F.S.

41   See *S & T Anchorage, Inc. v. Lewis, 575 So.2d 696 (Fla. 3d DCA 1991), reminding us that an association, like any other corporation, is prohibited from performing ultra vires acts.*

42   §720.3075 (1), F.S.

43   §720.3075 (2), F.S.

44   §617.0202, F.S.

45   §617.01401 (1), F.S.

46   *S & T Anchorage, Inc. v. Lewis, supra note 40; Wenger v. Breakwater Homeowners' Ass'n, supra note 28.*

The articles of incorporation may establish a corporation for profit or a corporation not-for-profit to be the homeowners association. Under most circumstances the articles of incorporation establish a "corporation not-for-profit" under Chapter 617 of the Florida Statutes. A corporation not-for-profit is not tax exempt, but it is a corporation where no part of the income may be distributed to the members, directors, or officers of the association.[47] Every corporation not-for-profit has all of the powers granted by the Florida Not For Profit Corporation Act (Chapter 617 of the Florida Statutes) except as otherwise limited by the articles of incorporation themselves.[48] The articles of incorporation become effective and the homeowners association may begin to operate when the articles are filed with the Division of Corporations.[49]

1.8   Bylaws. The articles of incorporation of the homeowners association define the association's basic structure and its areas of responsibility. The bylaws establish the procedures for the internal governance of the association and the procedures carrying out the responsibilities of the association.[50] They define the powers and the manner for exercising those powers by the board of directors and by each of the homeowners association's officers. Stated differently, the operation of the association is governed by the bylaws of the association.[51]

When creating the bylaws, there is a substantial amount of discretion available to establish the specific procedures which the homeowners association will follow. There are some provisions in the law, however, that mandate specific operational procedures for the association, and the bylaws must be consistent with these statutory requirements. Among these requirements are restrictions on the use of proxies, financial reporting obligations by the association, the requirement that all board meetings be open to the members of the association, and the requirement that notice be posted for all board meetings. The law also requires that certain records of the association be open to parcel owners.[52]

Because a portion of these mandatory requirements may not physically be within the bylaws, the board of directors and the association officers must be aware that portions of the operational requirements may be found in the statute and not as a part of the bylaws actually attached to

---

47   §617.01401 (5), F.S.
48   §617.0302, F.S.; *Orlando Orange Grove Co. v. Hale, supra note 28.*
49   §617.0203 (1), F.S. For associations created after October 1, 1995, the governing documents must be recorded in the official records of the county in which the community is located. §720.303 (1), F.S.
50   *Heron at Destin West Beach and Bay Resort Condominium Ass'n, Inc. v. Osprey at Destin West and Bay Resort Condominium Ass'n, Inc., 94 So.2d 623 (Fla. 1st DCA 2012).*
51   §617.01401 (3) and §617.0206, F.S.
52   §720.303, F.S.

the homeowners association documents. The procedural rights established by the bylaws are for the benefit of the members of the association, and non-members do not have standing to require that the association abide by its bylaws.[53]

1.9 Rules and Regulations. The supplemental restrictions authorized by the association bylaws and statute are traditionally referred to as the "rules and regulations." They are common in other forms of planned residential communities such as condominiums, cooperatives, and mobile home parks, and their role in homeowners associations is recognized by the statute.[54] The bylaws of the association may provide for the authority to adopt the rules and regulations and may set out the procedures to follow when adopting them.[55] The law governing homeowners associations specifically authorizes the adoption of rules governing the access to the official records of the association,[56] the taping and videotaping of meetings of the membership and the board of directors,[57] the procedure for conspicuously providing notice of membership meetings,[58] and the right of members to speak at meetings of the board of directors.[59]

The rules and regulations of the homeowners association are similar to the recorded declaration of covenants, but they are not clothed with the strong presumption of validity and enforceability that accompany recorded restrictions.[60] The rules of the homeowners association are considered a part of its official records[61] and the law requires a standard of reasonableness to ensure their enforceability.[62]

1.10 Priority and Consistency of the Documents. Each of the documents which make up the governing documents of the community and support the operation of the homeowners association are designed to interrelate and complement each other for the benefit of association members and parcel owners. Each of these documents should be consistent with the others and should be interpreted to carry out the common scheme

---

53   *Backus v. Smith, 363 So.2d 786,787 (Fla. 1st DCA 1978).*

54   *See §720.303 (4) (e) and §720.304 (1), F.S.*

55   §617.01401 (3) and §617.0206, F.S.

56   §720.303 (5) (c), F.S.

57   §720.306 (5), F.S.

58   §720.306 (10), F.S.

59   §720.303 (2)(b), F.S.

60   See *Eastpointe Property Owners' Ass'n v. Cohen, 505 So.2d 518, 520 (Fla. 4th DCA 1987) where actions by the board of directors were deemed valid provided they were not prohibited by the articles of incorporation or bylaws and were deemed reasonable actions designed to further the community concept. See also Bay Island Towers, Inc. v. Bay Island-Siesta Ass'n, 316 So.2d 574 (Fla. 2d DCA 1975).*

61   §720.303 (4) (e), F.S.

62   §720.304 (1), F.S.; see also *Eastpointe Property Owners' Ass'n v. Cohen, supra note 58.*

of the community.[63] When an apparent inconsistency is identified within a single document or between two of the governing documents, the inconsistent provisions should be reconciled,[64] or the provisions should be interpreted in such a way as to leave both provisions in effect and consistent with one another.[65]

When it is not possible to resolve an inconsistency between two different documents governing the community, then the provision in the highest priority document will prevail.[66] The document with the highest priority is the declaration of covenants, and its provisions will prevail over inconsistent provisions in other documents.[67] In descending order, the articles of incorporation for the homeowners association have the next highest priority after the declaration.[68] They are followed in descending order by the bylaws of the association and the duly adopted rules and regulations.[69] When a provision in any of the documents is inconsistent with state, federal, or local laws, the inconsistency in the community documents is invalidated in favor of the law.

1.11   Minutes and Records. A record of all meetings of the membership and the board of directors must be made in a businesslike manner and in written form or in a form that is capable of being converted to a written format within a reasonable period of time.[70] The board of directors is the custodian of all the official records of the homeowners association including all meeting minutes. The minutes of the association meetings become the prima facie evidence of the activities at the meetings, and they are usually held to be the best evidence of what they purport to show as to the association business that was conducted.[71]

The official records consist of all of the documents creating and governing the homeowners association. These include copies of plans, permits, warranties, and other items provided by the developer. They include the articles of incorporation, bylaws, deed restrictions, and the

---

63   *Holiday Pines Prop. Owners v. Wetherington, 596 So.2d 84, 87 (Fla. 4th DCA 1992).*

64   *Whitley v. Royal Trails Property Owners' Ass'n, Inc., 910 So.2d 381, 385 (Fla. 5th DCA 2005).*

65   "A restrictive covenant must be read in the context of the entire document in which it is contained." *Franklin v. White Egret Condominium, Inc., 358 So.2d 1084, 1087 (Fla. 4th DCA 1977). See also Flamingo Ranch Estates, Inc. v. Sunshine Ranches Homeowners, Inc., 303 So.2d 665 (Fla. 4th DCA 1974).*

66   *Koplowitz v. Imperial Towers Condominium, Inc., 478 So.2d 504 (Fla. 4th DCA 1985); San Souci v. Division of Fla. Land Sales and Condominiums, 421 So.2d 623 (Fla. 1st DCA 1982).*

67   *S & T Anchorage, Inc. v. Lewis, supra note 40.*

68   The bylaws may not be inconsistent with the articles of incorporation. §617.0206, F.S.

69   *Heron at Destin West Beach and Bay Resort Condominium Ass'n, Inc. v. Osprey at Destin West and Bay Resort Condominium Ass'n, Inc., supra note 49; Beachwood Villas Condominium v. Poor, 448 So.2d 1143 (Fla. 4th DCA 1984); Hidden Harbour Estates, Inc. v. Basso, 393 So.2d 637 (Fla. 4th DCA 1981).*

70   §720.303 (3), F.S.; see also *Fletcher's Cyclopedia on Corporations, Corporate Meetings and Elections, §2012.*

71   *Wimbledon Townhouse Condominium I, Ass'n, Inc. v. Wolfson, 510 So.2d 1106, 1108 (Fla. 4th DCA 1987); Gentry-Futch Co. v. Gentry, 90 Fla. 595, 609, 106 So. 473 (Fla. 1925).*

current rules and regulations governing the community. The official records include the accounting and financial records of the association and all contracts, management agreements, and leases to which the association is a party or under which it is obligated. The records also include the association insurance policies and a current roster of parcel owners.[72]

The board of directors must ensure that the minutes and other records of the homeowners association are properly maintained and available for inspection by the members and their authorized representatives. (See 6.6.) The minutes of the membership meetings, meetings of the board of directors, and most other records of the association must be maintained for a minimum period of seven (7) years.[73]

1.12 Directory of Homeowners. Although much of the information about homeowners maintained in the association records is confidential (see 6.6) and cannot be released without the consent of the owner, community directories are permitted. The directory may include the name of the individual home owner; the identification of the lot or parcels owned by the individual members of the association; the address of the property; the mailing addresses that the owners use to receive notices and other information from the homeowners association; and their telephone numbers.[74]

With the approval from the owners, the directory of homeowners may also include the owners' e-mail addresses, emergency contact information, and other personal information. Approval from a homeowner to use this additional personal information, however, must be in writing, and verbal consent by the owner cannot be relied upon to include the additional information in the community directory.[75]

1.13 Community Association Management. The managers of homeowners associations having more than ten (10) parcels or having an annual budget in excess of $100,000.00 or more are required to be licensed by the Department of Business and Professional Regulation.[76] To be certified as a community association manager, an individual must demonstrate good moral character and pass an examination administered by the Department prior to obtaining a license.

The Department sets the standards for the application, examination, and revocation of the licenses for those who wish to serve as managers of residential communities in Florida, and a licensed community association

---

72   §720.303 (3), F.S.
73   *Id.*
74   §720.303 (5) (c) 5., F.S.
75   *Id.*
76   §468.431 (2), F.S.

manager must comply with the provisions of Florida's residential housing laws in the course of providing management services to the community.[77] A licensed manager is required to participate in the continuing education prescribed by the Department in order to be eligible for renewal of the license,[78] and a manager must comply with the limitations placed on the services by the Florida Supreme Court. [79]

No person is permitted to perform the services of a community manager for compensation unless properly licensed. The community manager is considered an agent for the community when acting within the scope of authority authorized by law, and the manager is expected to discharge his or her duties loyally, skillfully, and diligently; dealing honestly and fairly; in good faith; with care and full disclosure to the association; accounting for all funds; and not charging unreasonable or excessive fees.[80] For members of the board of administration of a homeowners association, their fiduciary duty to the unit owners requires the board to employ only a licensed community manager where licensure is required.[81]

"Community association management" includes activities for remuneration involving the control and disbursement of funds, the preparation of budgets or other financial documents, assistance with the notice and conduct of association meetings, coordination of maintenance for the residential development, and other day-to-day services. A person who performs clerical or ministerial functions under the direct supervision and control of a licensed manager does not need to be licensed. A person charged only with performing the maintenance of a homeowners association who does not assist in any management activities also does not need to be licensed by the Department.[82]

In a community that employs a licensed manager, an individual parcel owner is not a third-party beneficiary of the agreement between the homeowners association and the community manager or management company.[83] Similarly, an individual parcel owner may not withhold the payment of a validly levied assessment to the association when a portion of the payment is being made to a manager or management company that is not properly licensed.[84]

---

77   §468.436 (2) (b) 7., F.S.

78   See generally §468.433, F.S. and §61B-55.006, F.A.C.

79   *The Florida Bar re Advisory Opinion—Activities of Community Ass'n Managers, 681 So.2d 1119 (Fla. 1996).*

80   §468.4334 (1), F.S.

81   §61B-23.001 (4), F.A.C.

82   §468.431 (2), F.S.

83   *Greenacre Properties, Inc. v. Rao, 933 So.2d 19 (Fla. 2d DCA 2006).*

84   *Gerecitano v. Barrwood Homeowners Ass'n, Inc., 882 So.2d 424 (Fla. 4th DCA 2004).*

1.14 Automated External Defibrillator. A homeowners association is permitted to maintain an automated external defibrillator device in the community for use in medical emergencies, and the association is immune from liability when the device is used as long as it is properly maintained, appropriate training has been provided to association employees, and the local emergency medical services director has been notified of the placement of the device in the community.[85] If the defibrillator device is placed in the community, the association's insurer may not require the association to purchase medical malpractice insurance and cannot exclude the use of the device from coverage under the association's general liability insurance coverage.[86]

1.15 The Legal Advisor. With the law come the lawyers, and they can be an important advisor to every board of administration. Almost every community has one or more retired lawyers, or one or more non-lawyers who have knowledge of the law governing community association, each of whom is willing to offer their advice and counsel to the board of directors without charge. Such advice may not be a bargain for the board receiving it. Relying on a wrong answer under such circumstances may be particularly hazardous to the board of directors, since its members are ultimately responsible for the consequences of the advice. (See 3.6.)

Each community should have a legal advisor knowledgeable in the law governing community associations. When the need arises, the board should call upon its counsel to render opinions for clarity and for guidance on matters affecting the community. The board of directors has met its responsibilities and abided by its fiduciary relationship when it asks for and relies upon the opinions of its attorney.[87] When receiving legal advice and to ensure its permanency, the opinions should be in writing and should be made a part of the association's permanent records.

To avoid unnecessary expense, a recommended practice followed by many communities is the maintenance of a book, or index, of legal opinions for use by future boards of administration facing similar problems. Written opinions also provide insulation for the board that has relied upon them, or has acted based on their direction.[88] The community and the board of administration will benefit from the skill and professional expertise offered by a competent attorney when the advice is appropriately sought and correctly followed.

---

85   §768.1325 (3), F.S.

86   §768.1325 (6), F.S.

87   §617.0830 (2), F.S.

88   *Id.*

2
Meetings of the Membership

2.1   General. Membership meetings are an essential part of a successfully operating homeowners association. The membership meetings provide association members the opportunity to select community leaders and a forum to adopt and approve association financial policies, make changes in the governing documents, handle items of special business involving the membership, and address other matters for the general welfare of the community.

If proper procedures are implemented and followed, membership meetings can deal with the most controversial subjects and still end with productive results. Unless the association bylaws provide a lower number, thirty (30) percent of the voting interests in the homeowners association must be present at a membership meeting to constitute a quorum.[1] For purposes of establishing a quorum, parcel owners attending in person and by general and limited proxy may be counted,[2] although the participation of those represented by proxy is restricted. (See 2.5.)

In some circumstances, owners may take action by written agreement, without a meeting, when it is expressly permitted by the articles of incorporation, the bylaws, or the law requiring the action. In all other cases, actions requiring parcel owner approval must take place at meetings of the association membership that are properly called and conducted. [3]

2.2   Annual and Regular Meetings. All homeowners associations are required to hold at least one regular membership meeting each year. This meeting is referred to as the "annual meeting," and the date, time, and place for it will likely be set forth in the bylaws of the association, or it will be set by the board of directors in the manner required in the bylaws and consistent with the requirements of Chapter 720 of the Florida Statutes.[4] (See 2.4.) Upon the request of a physically disabled person who has the right to attend a meeting of the membership, the meeting must be held at location that is accessible to physically disabled persons.[5]

A well-planned annual meeting will maximize the opportunities to provide information to members of the association and to receive their input, suggestions, and complaints. The annual meeting of members often presents the only periodic opportunity that individual owners have to review the affairs of their homeowners association, and any and all proper

---

1   §720.306 (1), F.S.
2   §720.306 (1) and (8), F.S.
3   §617.0701 (4), F.S.
4   §720.306 (2), F.S.
5   §720.306 (1) (a), F.S.

business of the association can be transacted at the annual meeting. Unless otherwise provided in the governing documents of the association, the election of directors must be held at, or in conjunction with, the annual meeting of the membership.[6] (See 2.10.)

2.3 Special Meetings.
From time to time, members of the homeowners association or the board of directors may find it necessary to hold special members' meetings. Special meetings are limited in their scope and purpose, and the notice to the members for a special meeting must include a description of the purpose for which the meeting is called.[7]

A special meeting of the association membership must be held when called by the board of directors or when at least ten (10) percent of the total voting interests of the association request a special meeting unless a different percentage of the membership is stated in the governing documents. The business conducted at a special meeting of the members is limited to the purpose or purposes described in the notice for the meeting.[8]

2.4 Content of Meeting Notice.
Notice of all membership meetings of the homeowners association must be mailed, delivered, or electronically transmitted to the members not less than fourteen (14) days prior to the meeting,[9] and an affidavit executed by the person providing the notice must be filed with the records of the association as evidence that the notice was given as required.[10] (See Form 10.1–1.) The notice for a membership meeting, whether annual or special, must contain the date, time, and place at which the meeting will be held.[11] If the meeting is a special meeting, the notice must include a description of the purpose or purposes for which the meeting has been called.[12] The notice of meeting must be electronically transmitted or mailed with postage paid to the address of each member shown in the association's records,[13] and the notice is effective when mailed.[14]

In a well-run community, the giving of notice will include, at minimum, the notice, an agenda of the business to be covered, and a proxy

---

6   §720.306 (2) and (9), F.S.
7   §720.306 (4), F.S.
8   §720.306 (2), F.S.
9   Where notice was not provided as the law required, "(t)he action of the court . . . holding the . . . meeting . . . illegal and the action taken null and void . . . was warranted by the evidence. . . ." *Gentry-Futch Co. v. Gentry, 90 Fla. 595, 608, 106 So. 473 (Fla. 1925).*
10   §720.306 (5), F.S.
11   §720.306 (2) and (4), F.S.
12   §720.306 (4), F.S.
13   §617.0141 (1), F.S.
14   §617.0141 (3), F.S.

form for the convenience of members who cannot attend in person. As a final option, the notice can be accompanied by reports of committees, reports by the association's president, or reports by the management company. If amendments to the governing documents are to be considered at the meeting, then copies of the amendments should be included with the notice. Finally, it may be helpful to include a general letter of explanation about the business to be discussed at the membership meeting and procedures to be followed during the course of the meeting.

The notice of each meeting is given by or at the direction of the president, secretary, or other officer or person assigned the responsibility of providing notice.[15] Notice of a meeting can be waived by a written waiver of notice either before or after a meeting. Attendance of a member at a meeting, either in person or by proxy, constitutes a waiver of notice unless the member attends solely for purpose of objecting, at the beginning of the meeting, to the lack of notice or the transaction of business at the meeting.[16]

2.5   Proxies. The bylaws for most homeowners associations permit absent parcel owners to participate and vote in membership meetings by proxy. Florida law also authorizes the use of proxies by a parcel owner but places certain restrictions on their use. No proxy is valid for more than ninety (90) days, and a proxy may be used only at the meeting for which it was given and any lawfully adjourned meetings thereof.[17] (See 2.15.) The proxy may be general in nature or very limited, restricting the person designated to vote it and allowing little discretion when representing the absent member. (See Forms 10.1–3 and 10.1–4.) Proxies are authorized for purposes of determining the presence of a quorum at all meetings of the membership,[18] and, unless otherwise restricted by the association bylaws, the use of proxies is permitted in the election of directors.[19] (See 2.10.)

To be valid, the proxy must identify the person who will vote the proxy at the meeting. The identification may be made by name or by designating a specific officer of the association, such as the president or secretary. The proxy must (1) be dated, (2) state the date, time, and place of the meeting for which the proxy is given, and (3) be signed by the person who is authorized to grant the proxy.[20] A proxy is revocable at any

---

15   §720.303 (1) and §720.306 (2) and (3), F.S.
16   §617.0701 (5) (a) and (b), F.S.
17   §720.306 (7) and (8), F.S.
18   §720.306 (1), F.S.
19   §720.306 (9), F.S.
20   §720.306 (8), F.S.

time at the pleasure of the person who executes it, and if the proxy form expressly permits, any proxy holder may appoint, in writing, a substitute to act in place of the proxy holder.[21]

The bylaws of most homeowners associations require that the proxies be returned to the secretary or other officer of the association prior to the meeting. The appointment of a proxy is effective when received by the secretary or other officer authorized to tabulate votes. An executed telegram or cablegram transmitted by a voting member of the association or a photographic, photostatic, facsimile, or equivalent reproduction of a proxy form is a sufficient proxy.[22]

2.6 Conducting the Meeting. Conducting a fair and successful membership meeting is the responsibility of the presiding officer or chairman. The chairman must set and maintain the proper tenor for the meeting and, as chairman, must at all times be fair, impartial, and neutral on each issue that comes before the meeting. The goal of the chairman should be to conduct an open and impartial membership meeting without regard to the outcome on specific votes or motions.[23]

In addition to setting an example of basic courtesy and fairness, the chairman must also be familiar with proper parliamentary procedures used for conducting the membership meeting. By following proper procedures, the chairman can allow the meeting to proceed with full participation of all members but without argument or disruption.[24] Conducting a successful meeting requires the assurance that all members wishing to participate can do so and that members wishing to make motions or debate an issue will have the appropriate opportunity.

Debate or remarks by individual members are protected by law[25] and should be limited or cut off only in extreme circumstances or when the remarks are being made at an improper point on the agenda. It is not unusual to find one or more individual members who will attempt to be disruptive, either intentionally or because they feel strongly on a particular issue. In such circumstances, the chairman must remain courteous, patient, and composed. The disruptive member desiring to be heard should be guided to the correct part of the agenda for his or her remarks and advised

---

21   *Id.*

22   §607.0722 (2), F.S.

23   "Aside from express regulations, all that is necessary is that the meeting be conducted by the proper persons, with fairness and good faith towards all who are entitled to take part, and in such a way as to enable them to express their vote upon questions coming before the meeting." *Fletcher's Cyclopedia on Corporations, Corporate Meetings and Elections, §2012.*

24   *Abbey Properties Co., Inc. v. Presidential Insurance Co., 119 So.2d 74, 77 (Fla. 2d DCA 1960); 18A Am. Jur. 2d, Corporations, §986.*

25   §720.306 (6), F.S.

how to make them in an appropriate and dignified fashion.[26] (See 2.12 and 2.13.)

2.7 Debate. Debate begins after a motion has been made, seconded, and stated by the presiding officer to the membership meeting. Each individual desiring to debate a motion must first be recognized by the chairman of the meeting,[27] and a member should not be permitted to speak a second time on the issue until all persons desiring to be heard the first time have had an opportunity to speak. The meeting chairman may bring debate to a close after the matter under consideration has been reasonably discussed if the strict rules of parliamentary procedure are not being followed.[28]

Members' debate must be confined to the specific issue before the meeting. Debate must be presented in a respectful manner so as to avoid issues of personalities and personal attacks. The maker of the motion, or the person presenting the subject, is the member allowed to speak last, but each member who has followed the proper procedures has the right to speak for at least three (3) minutes on any item.[29] No debate on a motion is in order after the vote has been taken and announced by the presiding officer and the item is no longer under consideration. During debate, it is permissible for a member to ask questions when another person is debating the issue, but all questions must be asked through the chairman. If the speaker is willing to yield to the question, then the member desiring to ask the question may do so.[30]

All main motions properly seconded are debatable as are motions to postpone a matter indefinitely and motions to rescind an action or to ratify an action. A motion to reconsider is debatable if the motion that is being reconsidered was debatable at the time it was made. Motions and matters of privilege, motions to waive the rules, motions to adjourn and to recess, and certain other incidental and subsidiary motions are not debatable.[31]

2.8 Matters Out of Order. The bylaws for many homeowners associations specifically adopt Robert's Rules of Order for use at association meetings. If the bylaws do not do so, the board of directors

---

26 To be valid, procedures must be reasonable and not arbitrary, and they must not be unreasonable in their practical application. See *Conlee Construction Co. v. Cay Construction Co.,* 221 So.2d 792, 796–797 *(Fla. 4th DCA 1969).*

27 *Robert's Rules of Order Newly Revised (1990), §42.*

28 *Fletcher's Cyclopedia on Corporations, Corporate Meetings and Elections, §2012.*

29 §720.306 (6), F.S.

30 *Robert's Rules of Order Newly Revised (1990), §3.*

31 *Robert's Rules of Order Newly Revised (1990), Charts, Tables and Lists, §II.*

or membership may specify the rules of procedure to be followed. The rules of parliamentary procedure establish an order for business of the meeting and the manner in which business is presented and disposed of by those in attendance at the meeting. The rules of parliamentary procedure also establish an order of priority for motions that may be made by a participant at a meeting. A matter can be out of order when it is presented at the wrong time[32] or when it is presented in the wrong way.[33] Under either of these circumstances, it is the prerogative and the duty of the presiding officer to rule the matter out of order.

A main motion is out of order when another main motion is already pending or when the main motion is on a subject that should arise under a different order of business on the agenda. A motion will also be out of order when a motion of higher priority or of "higher dignity" is already being considered by the meeting. A member may be out of order if the member is either not properly recognized by the chairman or if the member seeks to make a dilatory or frivolous motion.

To call a point of order to demand that the proper order of business be followed is a privileged matter or motion for any member. When claiming a point of order, it is proper for the member to rise and state the point. It does not require a second to be considered by the chairman. A question or point of order cannot be amended by another member and must be decided by the presiding officer without debate.[34]

The presiding officer may seek consultation with the meeting's legal advisor or parliamentarian before ruling on the point of order, but it is the presiding officer's duty to enforce the rules and the order of business of the meeting without debate or unnecessary delay.[35] It is the right of every member who notices a departure from the rules or from the order of business to insist upon proper enforcement.[36]

2.9   Voting and Vote Tabulations. Each member of the homeowners association is assigned a "voting interest" in the association pursuant to the governing documents of the association.[37] The process of voting is the method of expressing the collective will of these membership interests

---

32   *Robert's Rules of Order Newly Revised (1990), §40.*
33   *Robert's Rules of Order Newly Revised (1990), §5.*
34   *Robert's Rules of Order Newly Revised (1990), §23.*
35   *Id.*
36   *Id.; See also Hagan v. Sabal Palms, Inc., 186 So.2d 302 (Fla. 2d DCA 1966) and Loch Haven Homeowners' Ass'n v. Nelle, 389 So.2d 697 (Fla. 2d DCA 1980) recognizing an individual homeowner's standing to challenge board action or to enforce covenants.*
37   §720.301 (13), F.S.

in the affairs of the homeowners association.[38] There are five basic ways for that voting process to take place; (1) by "general consent," (2) by "voice vote," (3) by "show of hands," (4) by "roll call," and (5) by "ballot."[39] Each type of voting has its appropriate place at a membership meeting, and each type can be used effectively at a well run meeting of the members.[40] Use of an inappropriate voting method, on the other hand, can result in disruption or in an actual breakdown of the meeting.

Voting by "general consent" is most often used when there is no objection to an issue before the membership. The chairman of the meeting will simply ask if there is any objection to the motion on the floor, and, if there is none, the chairman will declare that the motion is approved. "Voice voting" is used when an issue before the meeting is relatively non-controversial. The chairman of the meeting will ask for those in favor of the issue to say "aye" and for those who are opposed to the motion to say "no." The chairman will then rule on which group carried the motion. A voice vote should be taken only when the motion requires a majority vote, and, if a member disagrees with the ruling of the chairman on the voice vote, the member may request a count by one of the other voting methods.[41]

Voting by "show of hands" is often a simple sight verification of a voice vote and does not necessarily require that an actual count of hands be made. An exact count of the hands can be made, but an exact count by either roll call or by ballot is more correct. A "roll call" vote requires that the name of each member present be called, allowing for a response of "yes" or "no" to be made on the issue. Because a roll call vote is both time consuming and tedious, it is rarely used at association meetings. Voting by "ballot" is the preferred alternative when an exact vote tabulation is desired.[42] (See Form 10.1–7.)

The final results when voting by general consent, by voice vote, or by a show of hands is determined by the chairman of the meeting.[43] Tabulation of a roll call is a simple summation of the individual responses

---

38   18A *Am. Jur. 2d, Corporations, §999; "Corporations must be allowed to function under majority control, so long as the majority does no actual wrong to the minority or to others." Coleman v. Plantation Golf Club, Inc.,* 212 So.2d 806, 808 (Fla. 4th DCA 1968).

39   *Robert's Rules of Order Newly Revised (1990), §44.*

40   The procedural requirements governing the association's role on behalf of its members are appropriately political matters to be addressed within the organization and political framework of the association. See *Eberwein v. Coral Pine Condominium One,* 431 So.2d 616, 618 (Fla. 4th DCA 1983).

41   18A *Am. Jur. 2d, Corporations, §991.*

42   18A *Am. Jur. 2d, Corporations, §1000.*

43   "[A] presiding officer cannot wrongfully declare the result of a vote or arbitrarily refuse to entertain or put motions. Moreover, a chairman's announcement of the results of an election contrary to the vote actually cast has no legal effect on the result." 18A *Am. Jur. 2d, Corporations, §991.*

of members, while determining the results from a vote by ballot is by a separate, organized counting procedure which can be simplified significantly if the board has properly organized for the count. When counting, a ballot containing votes for too many board members must be disallowed, while a ballot that does not vote for all available choices is counted for the choices actually made.[44]

When deciding who will actually tabulate the ballots at a membership meeting, the board should keep in mind two basic considerations. The first consideration is the number of votes to be cast and the number of individuals that will be needed to ensure a prompt and accurate tabulation of the votes. The second consideration is the nature of the election and the issues involved. It is helpful to have representatives of both sides of controversial issues involved in the count to remove any doubt on the validity of the results. On some occasions, inspectors of election are actually elected by the membership, but, in most circumstances, the inspectors may simply be appointed by the chairman of the meeting.[45]

Generally, voting and voting rights are covered by the association's bylaws; however, bylaw provisions that conflict with provisions of Florida law are invalid.[46]

2.10 Election of the Board of Directors. The election of the board of directors of the homeowners association is required to be held at, or in conjunction with, the annual meeting of members.[47] All members of the association are eligible to serve on the board of directors, and any member may nominate himself or herself as a candidate for the board of directors at the meeting where the election is to be held unless the election process allows a candidate to be nominated in advance of the meeting.[48]

The association may employ any form of voting process permitted by the governing documents, and, unless otherwise prohibited by the documents, members of the association may vote by proxy.[49] If ballots are used in the election process, the balloting, by its parliamentary nature, is a secret voting procedure.[50] (See 2.11.)

---

44   *Fletcher's Cyclopedia on Corporations, Corporate Meetings and Elections, §2017.*
45   *Fletcher's Cyclopedia on Corporations, Corporate Meetings and Elections, §2018; 18A Am. Jur. 2d, Corporations, §1008 and §1009.*
46   *C.A. Cavendes, Sociedad Financiera v. Florida National Banks, 566 F. Supp. 254, 258 (M.D. Fla. 1982) citing Gentry - Futch v. Gentry, supra note 8, pages 477–478.*
47   §720.306 (2), F.S.
48   §720.306 (9), F.S.An election is not required unless more candidates are nominated than vacancies exist.
49   §720.306 (8), F.S.
50   *Robert's Rules of Order Newly Revised (1990), §44; Fletcher's Cyclopedia on Corporations, Corporate Meetings and Elections, §2017.*

Any election dispute between a member and the association must be submitted by petition to mandatory binding arbitration with the Division of Florida Land Sales, Condominiums, and Mobile Homes.[51] The petition must set forth the nature of the dispute, and it must be resolved by the arbitrator on an expedited basis under the procedural rules of the Division.[52]

2.11 Board Elections by Ballot. When the governing documents permit election by ballot, the law provides basic procedures to ensure ballot secrecy and appropriate verification of eligible voting members.[53] The procedures require two envelopes—an inner envelope with no markings to hold the ballot that is delivered to the association in a second, outer envelope bearing identifying information reflecting (1) the name of the member casting the ballot, (2) the lot or parcel number of the member casting the ballot, and (3) the signature of the member submitting the ballot.[54]

When the tabulation begins, the eligibility of each member is confirmed by the identifying information on the outer envelope and a determination is made that no other ballot has been submitted by the owner. The inner envelopes are then taken out of the outer envelopes and placed with the other ballots for counting. If more than one (1) ballot is contained in an inner envelope, the ballots in the envelope shall be disqualified. Any votes received after the balloting is closed cannot be counted toward the totals in the election.[55]

Because all members of the homeowners association are eligible to serve as a member of the board of directors and all members may nominate themselves as candidates, the association must provide an appropriate opportunity for the nominations to occur prior to distributing the ballots.[56] (See 3.5.) If the governing documents do not specify a procedure for the nominations, the board should provide an appropriate procedure by rule to ensure that the opportunity authorized by statute is available to the membership. (See 3.1.)

---

51   §720.306 (9), F.S.
52   §§718.1255 (4) and (5), F.S.
53   §720.306 (8), F.S.
54   *Id.*
55   *Id.*
56   *Id.*

2.12 Decorum. Decorum for a successful meeting is built on mutual respect between the membership and the presiding officer of the meeting.[57] Members wishing to speak should be presented through the chairman of the meeting.[58] Members wishing to obtain the floor for any purpose should do so properly by seeking the recognition of the presiding officer. Once a member assumes the floor, the rules of debate should be obeyed, and all comments should be confined to the question before the meeting. Comments and statements relating to personal motives and to personalities should not be made and may be ruled out of order by the presiding officer.[59]

Proper decorum at a meeting is no more than the exercise of common courtesy and maintaining respect for the rights of others. To ensure that decorum is maintained, the presiding officer of the meeting should guide members through the proper order of business. The presiding officer must require that the rules be followed at all times. At the same time, the chairman must be both flexible and patient with members who are unfamiliar with the formal rules of parliamentary procedure.[60] The chairman should not permit conduct that is disruptive, tedious, or dilatory.

2.13 Speaking at Membership Meetings. It is the right of all association members and parcel owners to speak at any meeting of the membership with reference to all items open for discussion or included on the meeting agenda. The board of directors of the association may adopt reasonable rules governing the frequency, duration, and manner of member statements, but the rules must be in writing. The rules governing the right of members to speak may require an owner to submit a written request to speak prior to the meeting, and the rules must permit any parcel owner or member to speak for at least three (3) minutes on any item, provided that the member or owner has submitted a written request to do so prior to the meeting.[61]

---

57   "Aside from express regulations, all that is necessary is that the meeting be conducted by the proper persons, with fairness and good faith towards all who are entitled to take part, and in such a way as to enable them to express their vote upon questions coming before the meeting." *Fletcher's Cyclopedia on Corporations, Corporate Meetings and Elections, §2012.*

58   "The presiding officer of a . . . meeting has no authority to defeat the will of the majority by arbitrary rulings, since the will of the majority is binding on him when legally expressed. Thus, a presiding officer cannot wrongfully declare the result of a vote or arbitrarily refuse to entertain or put motions." 18A *Am Jur. 2d, Corporations, §991.*

59   *Robert's Rules of Order Newly Revised (1990), §42.*

60   *Id.*

61   §720.306 (6), F.S.

2.14 Recording and Taping Membership Meetings. Any

parcel owner may tape-record or videotape meetings of the association membership. The right to record meetings may be subject to restrictions imposed by the board of directors, provided that the restrictions are reasonable and have been adopted as rules of the homeowners association by the board of directors.[62] Examples of such reasonable rules would include restrictions requiring prior notice by the member desiring to make a recording, restrictions requiring installation of the recording equipment prior to the commencement of the meeting, and restrictions on recording equipment that produce distracting sound or light emissions.

Rules that significantly impair the recording privileges, however, would not comply with the clear language in the law and will not be sustained in court. Restrictions such as those prescribing a location for recording devices that would not permit the business of the meeting to be recorded or that would result in unreasonable interference with the tapings make the privilege meaningless and effectively deny the privilege. It is a well-established principle that the meaning of the statute must be given its plain and ordinary interpretation, and restrictions may not have the effect of eliminating the right of owners to record proceedings as the statute intends.[63]

2.15 Adjournment to a Different Time. It is permissible to adjourn

a membership meeting for the purpose of reconvening to conclude the business of the meeting at a different time and place. Unless the association bylaws require otherwise, the adjournment of a meeting to a different date, time, and place must be announced at the meeting before an adjournment is taken.[64] Otherwise, notice for the reconvened portion of the meeting must be posted in a conspicuous place in the community at least forty-eight (48) hours in advance of the meeting, or, in the alternative, notice must be mailed or delivered to each member at the last known address seven (7) days before the reconvened meeting.[65]

Any business that might have been transacted on the original date of the membership meeting may be transacted when the meeting is reconvened.[66] Special attention must be given to the proxies that have been

---

62   §720.306 (10), F.S.
63   *Winter v. Playa del Sol, Inc., 353 So.2d 598, 599 (Fla. 4th DCA 1977).*
64   §720.306 (7), F.S.
65   §720.306 (7) and §720.303 (2), F.S. For communities with more than one hundred (100) members, the bylaws may provide for a reasonable alternative to posting or mailing of notice. §720.303 (2), F.S.
66   §720.306 (7), F.S.; *Lake Forest Master Community Ass'n, Inc. v. Orlando Lake Forest Joint Venture, 10 So.3d 1187 (Fla. 5th DCA 2009).*

returned for the meeting, however, since the proxies expire ninety (90) days after the date of the meeting for which they were originally given.[67]

2.16 Smoking and the Clean Indoor Air Act. In November of 2002, Floridians approved a constitutional amendment banning smoking of all tobacco products in enclosed indoor locations where work is performed.[68] The definition of "work" includes all indoor meetings of the board of directors, committees of the board, and meetings of the membership, and accordingly, no smoking is permitted at these meetings. The definition is also sufficiently broad to include all indoor common areas of the community where work or service is performed by an officer, director, manager, employee, contractor, or volunteer, and the simple cleaning or maintenance of the enclosed common areas is sufficient to impose a ban on smoking within these areas.[69]

It is the responsibility of the board of directors to establish appropriate policies prohibiting smoking in enclosed indoor workplaces within the community, and policies may include the posting of "no smoking" signs as the board deems appropriate.[70] Persons violating the Clean Indoor Air Act are subject to a $100.00 fine for the first occurrence and a $500.00 fine for each subsequent occurrence.[71]

---

67   §720.306 (8), F.S.
68   §2, Article X, Constitution of Florida.
69   §386.203 (5) and (12), F.S.
70   §386.206 (2), F.S.
71   §386.208, F.S.

3
Board of Directors and Meetings of the Board

3.1 General. The operation and management of the community's affairs are vested in the homeowners association. The board of directors is responsible for carrying out the duties and responsibilities of the homeowners association.[1] To the extent that the association has control of the affairs and the property of the community, the board of directors has the responsibility to implement that authority.[2]

The board of directors must consist of three (3) or more individuals with the actual number fixed in accordance with the articles of incorporation.[3] Directors will serve for a term of one (1) year unless the articles of incorporation or the bylaws of the homeowners association provide for different terms of office.[4] Unless the governing documents provide to the contrary, members of the board of directors may not receive any fee or compensation from the performance of their duties as directors.[5] (See 4.11.)

The authority of the board of directors is comprehensive and includes all of the powers and duties enumerated in Chapter 617 of the Florida Statutes (Florida Not For Profit Corporation Act), as long as the powers are not inconsistent with the provisions of the documents governing the community and the homeowners association.[6]

3.2 Election and Selection. The articles of incorporation or the bylaws of the homeowners association must provide the manner for the selection and the election of the members of the board of directors.[7] Generally, there are two methods for selecting members to serve on the board. The first, and most common, is by election to the board by members of the association at an annual or special meeting.[8] (See 2.10 and 2.11.) The second method of selection is by appointment to the board of directors. The appointment may occur by the developer if the developer is still entitled to representation[9] or it may be by the remaining members of the board of directors when a vacancy on the board occurs between meetings of the membership.

When a vacancy arises on the board of directors between meetings of the membership, the remaining board members may select a new member by appointment. Vacancies on the board may be filled by the

---

1   §617.01401(2), F.S.
2   §617.0801, F.S.
3   §617.0803, F.S.
4   §617.0803 (3) and §617.0806, F.S.
5   §720.303 (12)(d), F.S.
6   §720.303 (1) and §617.0302, F.S.
7   §720.306 (9) and §617.0803 (3), F.S.
8   §720.306 (2), F.S.
9   §720.307 (1) and (2), F.S.

remaining board members even if the remaining members are less than a majority of the full board of directors.[10] The term of a board member appointed to fill a vacancy will continue for the unexpired term of his or her predecessor in office. At the expiration of the term, a replacement member to the board can be elected by the membership.[11]

When a new member is elected or appointed to the board of directors, the new member is required to certify in writing to the secretary of the association that he or she has read the association's governing documents, will work to uphold the documents and policies of the community, and will faithfully discharge his or her fiduciary responsibilities to the community.[12] In the alternative, a certificate of satisfactory completion of an education course approved by the Division of Florida Condominiums, Timeshares, and Mobile Homes may be provided in lieu of the certificate to the secretary. A board member who fails to timely file the required written certification or education certificate within ninety (90) days of being elected or appointed is suspended from service on the board until the member complies with the certificate requirement. The certificate provided by each new board member must be retained in the association records for at least five (5) years or for the duration of the member's uninterrupted tenure on the board, whichever is longer.[13]

3.3 Failure to Fill Board Vacancies. If a homeowners association fails to fill vacancies on the board of directors sufficient to constitute a quorum, any member of the association may apply to the circuit court for the appointment of a receiver to manage the affairs of the association.[14] At least thirty (30) days before applying to the court, the member must advise the association and its other members of the intended action by posting notice in a conspicuous place in the community and by mailing notice to the association by certified or registered mail.[15] If the association fails to fill a sufficient number of vacancies within thirty (30) days so that a quorum of the board can be assembled, the member may proceed with the petition in circuit court.[16]

The appointment of a receiver in other circumstances rests within the sound discretion of the Circuit Court. These circumstances may arise in the presence of fraud, self-dealing, or the waste of a secured asset; and if

---

10   §720.306 (9), F.S.
11   *Id.*
12   §720.3033 (1) (a), F.S.
13   §720.3033 (1) (c), F.S.
14   §720.3053 (1), F.S.
15   §720.3053 (2), F.S.
16   §720.3053 (3), F.S.

the facts justify such an action, the judge may appoint a receiver under the equitable authority of the court.[17]

When a receiver is appointed by the court, the receiver is required to provide all members of the homeowners association with written notice of the appointment,[18] and the association is responsible for the salary of the receiver, court costs and attorney's fees, and all other costs of the receivership.[19] The receiver possesses all of the powers and duties of a duly constituted board of directors and serves until the homeowners association fills vacancies on the board sufficient to constitute a quorum.[20]

3.4   Eligibility. The articles of incorporation or bylaws of the homeowners association will specify and provide the eligibility requirements for the members of the board of directors. Florida's law does not require individual board members to be members of the association or residents of the state unless the articles of incorporation or bylaws impose these qualifications.[21] The law does, however, declare that all qualified members of the association are eligible to serve as a member of the board of directors, and any member may nominate himself or herself as a candidate for the board of directors at the meeting of members where the election is to be held.[22] A member is not qualified and is not eligible to serve as a member of the board if he or she is delinquent for more than 90 days in monetary obligations due to the association or has been convicted of an offense considered a felony under Florida law.[23]

When eligibility is limited to ownership and a parcel is owned jointly, each of the owners is qualified to serve on the board even though only one of the owners may be designated to exercise the parcel's voting rights. When a parcel is owned by a corporation or another type of artificial person such as a partnership or trust, determining the eligibility for a representative of the parcel to serve on the board of directors presents a unique dilemma. If the bylaws permit, the designated voting representative of the corporation may be eligible for the board. If eligibility is contingent upon association membership, then the parcel may be effectively excluded from offering a candidate for the board since a corporation cannot sit as a member of the board of directors.[24]

An exception to this eligibility standard is made when the lot or

---

17   *Metro-Dade Investments, Co. v. Granada Lakes Villas Condominium, Inc., 74 So.3d 593, 594 (Fla. 2d DCA 2011).*

18   §720.3053 (4), F.S. and §720.313, F.S.

19   §720.3053 (5), F.S.

20   §720.3053 (3), F.S.

21   §617.0802, F.S.

22   §720.306 (9), F.S.

23   §720.306 (9) (b), F.S. Eligibility is restored if a felon's civil rights have been restored for at least 5 years.

24   §720.306 (9), F.S.

parcel is owned by a trust. If a lot is owned by a trust and the grantors or beneficiaries of the trust occupy the parcel, then the occupants are considered members of the association and are eligible for service on the board of directors.[25]

Membership in the homeowners association passes with ownership of a parcel.[26] When a parcel is sold, the membership in the homeowners association is also transferred to the new owner. When ownership is an eligibility requirement for service on the board, transfer of a parcel will terminate the eligibility of an individual to serve on the board of directors and create a vacancy on the board at the time of sale.

3.5   Resignation, Recall, and Removal. A member of the board of directors may voluntarily resign at any time by delivery of his or her written notice of resignation to the board of directors, to its chairman, or to the homeowners association.[27] The resignation is effective when the notice is delivered unless the notice specifies a later effective date. When the resignation is effective at a later date, the remaining directors may fill the pending vacancy before the effective date, provided the successor does not take office until the vacancy is effective.[28] (See 3.2.) An association director who is charged with theft or embezzlement involving association funds or property is automatically removed from office,[29] and any director who solicits or accepts goods or services for his or her personal benefit while serving on the board is subject to immediate removal by the remaining members of the board.[30]

Any member of the board of directors may be recalled and removed with or without cause by a majority of the total voting interests in the homeowners association.[31] The recall may be by written agreement or by written ballot without a membership meeting, and the recall documentation must be served on the association by certified mail or by personal service.[32] When the recall documentation is received, the board of directors shall notice and hold a meeting within five (5) business days to certify the ballots or the recall agreement. Once the documentation is certified, the recall is effective immediately, and the director or directors

---

25   §617.0802 (2), F.S.
26   §720.301 (9) and (11), F.S.
27   §617.0807 (1), F.S.
28   §720.306 (9), F.S. and §617.0807 (2), F.S.
29   §720.3033 (4), F.S.
30   §720.3033 (4), F.S.An officer or board member is permitted to accept food to be consumed at a business meeting with a value of less than $25 or a service or good received in connection with trade fairs or education programs.
31   §720.303 (10) (a) 1, F.S.
32   §720.303 (10) (b) 1, F.S.

recalled shall turn over any and all property of the association in their possession within five (5) working days of the certification by the board.[33]

If the recall procedures remove less than a majority of the board of directors, the vacancy or vacancies created may be filled by an affirmative vote of the remaining directors. When the recall results in the removal of a majority or more of the board of directors, the vacancies shall be filled by the members voting in favor of the recall.[34] In such circumstances, the written recall agreement or recall ballots must list at least as many possible replacement directors as there are directors subject to recall, permitting the person executing the recall instrument or ballot to vote for the replacement of the directors subject to the recall.[35]

In the event that the board of directors determines to reject some or all of the recall votes and not to certify the recall, the board shall file a petition for binding arbitration for the resolution of the dispute with the Department of Business and Professional Regulation within five (5) days.[36] The minutes of the board meeting must identify the specific reason for rejecting a member's recall vote and the parcel number owned by the member whose vote is rejected.[37] The Department arbitrator is required to expedite consideration of the dispute and the matter is finalized when the final order of arbitration is issued.[38]

As an alternative recall procedure, when the community documents specifically permit, the association members may recall a board member or members by a vote at a membership meeting called by ten (10) percent of the voting interests of the association. After the membership vote approving the recall, the board is required to call a meeting with five (5) days to certify the results or proceed with arbitration.[39]

3.6 Fiduciary Relationship. The members of the board of directors and each officer of the homeowners association have a fiduciary relationship with the members of the association.[40] This fiduciary relationship imposes obligations of trust and confidence in favor of the association and its members. It requires each member of the board to act in good faith and in a manner he or she believes to be in the best interests of the members of the association. It means the board members must exercise

---

33   §720.303 (10) (b) 2, F.S.
34   §720.303 (10) (e), F.S.
35   §720.303 (10) (b) 5 and §720.303 (10) (i), F.S.
36   §720.303 (10) (d), F.S.
37   §720.303 (10) (h), F.S.
38   §720.303 (10) (d), F.S.
39   §720.303 (10) (c), F.S.
40   §720.303 (1), F.S.

the care and diligence of an ordinarily prudent person when acting for the community, and it requires each of them to act within the scope of their authority.[41]

Directors and officers of the association must devote enough time and effort to the performance of their duties to ensure that they are reasonably and faithfully carried out on behalf of the association. The fact that the homeowners association is a corporation not for profit, or that the members of the board are volunteers and unpaid, does not relieve them from the standards of trust and responsibility that the fiduciary relationship requires.[42] When confronted with an issue involving special expertise such as a question of law, building or construction matters, insurance or accounting questions, or other similar issues, the law also contemplates that the board of directors or an officer will seek the appropriate advice of a professional considered competent in the field and rely upon that advice provided.[43]

3.7   Indemnification. When directors and officers of the homeowners association are properly carrying out their duties within the scope of responsibility assigned to them, they may be indemnified by the association and its members when claims or suits are brought against them for their actions. The right of indemnification does not, however, extend to members of the board of directors appointed by the developer,[44] and association funds may not be used by a developer to defend actions filed against the developer or directors appointed by the developer even when the proceedings concern the operations of the developer-controlled association.[45]

The association is required to maintain insurance or a fidelity bond at the association's expense for all persons who control or disburse funds of the association, and the amount of the bond or insurance must be sufficient to cover the maximum amount of funds in the custody of the association or its management agent at any one time.[46] The "persons who control funds of the association" include all persons authorized to sign checks as well as the president, secretary and treasurer of the association.[47]

In fulfilling their duties and responsibilities, board members

---

41   §617.0830 (1), F.S.
42   §720.303 (1), F.S.
43   "In discharging his or her duties, a director may rely on information, opinions, reports or statements…, if prepared by: legal counsel, public accountants, or other persons as to matters the director reasonably believes are within the persons' professional or expert competence;"*See §617.0830 (2) (b), F.S.*
44   §617.0831, F.S.
45   §720.303 (8) (c), F.S.
46   §720.3033 (5), F.S.
47   *Id.A majority of the members present at a membership meeting may waive the requirement on an annual basis.*

and officers may utilize certain information provided by others when discharging duties on the association's behalf. Information, opinions, and reports from officers and employees of the association whom the director believes to be reliable and competent may be relied upon, and the advice and opinions of legal counsel and other professionals may also be appropriately used.[48]

3.8 Meetings of the Board.

Actions of the board of directors take place at meetings of the board. A meeting of the board of directors includes any gathering of a quorum of the members for the purpose of conducting homeowners association business. Meetings may be either a regular or special gathering, and they may be called by the chairman, the president, or any other persons who are authorized to do so by the bylaws of the association.[49] Unless the bylaws place a restriction on the place of the meeting, it may be held wherever the board of directors finds it necessary. The place may include the offices of the association's attorney, accountant, or manager or another location deemed appropriate by the board.[50] Upon the request of a physically disabled person who has the right to attend a meeting of the board, the meeting location must be accessible to physically disabled persons.[51]

Unless prohibited by the articles of incorporation or bylaws, the board of directors may permit any or all directors to participate in a meeting by means of real-time communication. Absent board members are permitted to participate fully in a board meeting via telephone, videoconferencing, or similar real-time electronic or video communication if conversations of the absent board member may be heard by the other members of the board and owners attending the meeting. A director participating in a board meeting in this manner is considered to be present at the meeting.[52] A director is not permitted to vote by proxy or by secret ballot at board meetings, except that directors may vote by secret ballot when electing officers of the homeowners association.[53]

A quorum of the board of directors consists of a majority of the members of the board established in the articles of incorporation or the bylaws.[54] When a quorum is present, the affirmative vote of a majority of the directors present is an act of the board unless the articles or bylaws

---

48 §617.0830 (2), F.S.
49 See generally §617.0820, §617.0824 (3), and §720.303 (2), F.S.
50 §617.0820 (1), F.S.
51 §720.303 (2) (a), F.S.
52 §617.0820 (4), F.S.
53 §720.303 (2), F.S.
54 §617.0824 (1), F.S. The articles of incorporation or the bylaws of the association may provide for a quorum of less than a majority but no fewer than one-third of the prescribed number of directors.

require the vote of a greater number of directors.[55] A director who is present when an action is taken is deemed to have agreed with the action unless he or she votes against the action or affirmatively abstains or objects at the beginning of the meeting to holding the meeting or transacting specified affairs at the meeting.[56] (See 3.6.) The minutes of the meeting should reflect the vote of each board member on each action taken at the meeting.

The law provides that the powers of the association are exercised by the board of directors,[57] and each board member is obligated to discharge the duties that have been assigned to the board.[58] The corporate law does not provide for a member of the board of directors to abstain on reasons of general principle, and board members should do so only when a conflict of interest actually exists.[59] The nature of the conflict and the reason for abstaining must be disclosed to the remaining members of the board and recorded in the minutes of the meeting.[60]

Florida's corporate law permits the board of directors to take action without a meeting if all of the board members consent to the action in writing unless the articles of incorporation or bylaws provide otherwise. The written consent will have the same effect as if a unanimous vote had been taken at a meeting. An action taken without a meeting of the board becomes effective when the last director signs the consent unless the consent specifies a different effective date.[61]

3.9   Notice to Board Members. There are two types of notice that must be given before a proper meeting of the board of directors of a homeowners association can be held. The first is for the individual members of the board, and the second is for the general association membership. The notice to members of the board of directors can be made by first-class mail, by personal delivery, by telegram, or by electronic transmission, and notice must be given at least two (2) days prior to the meeting itself. The provisions of the association's bylaws may provide for different notice requirements and for longer or shorter periods of time.[62] (See 3.10.)

Notice to board members for regular meetings of the board may be dispensed with unless notice is required by the articles of incorporation or

---

55   §617.0824 (3), F.S.
56   §720.303 (3) and §617.0824 (4), F.S.
57   §617.0801, F.S. and §720.303 (1), F.S.
58   §617.0830, F.S.
59   §617.0832, F.S. or §617.0822, F.S.
60   §720.303 (4) (f), F.S. and§ 617.0824 (4), F.S.
61   §617.0821, F.S.
62   §617.0822 (2), F.S.

bylaws,[63] and notice may be waived by board members who sign a waiver of notice either before or after the meeting.[64]

3.10 Notice to Association Members. Proper notice for all board meetings of the association must be provided,[65] and all meetings of the board must be open to the members of the homeowners association with two exceptions. Meetings between the board and its attorney with respect to proposed or pending litigation where the contents of the discussion would be governed by the attorney-client privilege may be closed to the membership,[66] and meetings of the board of directors that are held for the purpose of discussing personnel matters may also be closed.[67] Otherwise, the requirement for open meetings extends not only to meetings of the board but also to all committees of the board and executive councils which are carrying out a portion of the association's responsibilities.[68]

The law provides alternative methods for providing notice to the association membership. Notice of most board meetings must be conspicuously posted on the association property at least forty-eight (48) hours in advance of each meeting, except in an emergency. In the alternative, if notice is not posted, it must be mailed, electronically transmitted, or delivered to each member of the association at least seven (7) days before the meeting, except in an emergency. If the community is served by a closed-circuit television system, the notice may be given by broadcasting the notice at least four (4) times every broadcast hour of each day that a posted notice is otherwise required. In communities where the homeowners association has more than one hundred (100) members, the bylaws of the association may provide a reasonable alternative to the general notice requirements of posting or mailing of the notice.[69]

Special notice requirements apply when a board meeting is scheduled to consider assessments against parcels in the community or when changes in the rules and regulations that govern the use of parcels in the community will be considered. The written notice for board meetings scheduled to consider these topics must be provided to members at least fourteen (14) days prior to the meeting, and when an assessment it to be considered, the notice must so state and describe the nature of the assessment. When changes to the rules will be considered, the notice must

---

63   §617.0822 (1), F.S.
64   §617.0823, F.S.
65   §720.303 (2) (c), F.S.
66   §720.303 (2) (a), F.S.
67   §720.303 (2) (b), F.S.
68   §720.303 (2) (a), (b), and (c), F.S.
69   §720.303 (2) (c) 1, F.S.

contain a statement that the board is considering changes to the rules and regulations.[70]

3.11 Membership Participation. Members of the homeowners association have the right to attend all meetings of the board of directors and also have the right to speak before the board on all designated items on the meeting agenda.[71] Members also have the right to add items of business to the agenda of the board by written petition executed by twenty (20) percent or more of the total voting interests of the association. The item or items of business must be included on the agenda of the next regular or special meeting of the board, and a meeting must be held not later than 60 days following receipt of the membership petition to consider the item or items. [72] The board of directors is required to give all members fourteen (14) days' notice of the meeting at which the petitioned item or items will be addressed, but the board is not obligated to take any other action requested by the petition.[73]

The board of directors of the association is permitted to adopt written rules governing the rights of members to speak and the frequency and duration of the participation by members at board meetings.[74] Maintaining a regular portion of the agenda for membership comment helps to diffuse controversy and problems and permits the board of directors to have regular and orderly communications from members of the association. When considering the rules for member participation, the board should also consider how it can best be handled in an orderly fashion. A specific part of the agenda for member participation is, in most cases, a more preferable alternative to continuous member involvement throughout the full agenda of the board meeting.

Members are permitted to tape-record or videotape meetings of the board of directors, although the board may adopt reasonable rules to govern the taping.[75] (See 2.14.) Finally, notwithstanding other provisions of law, the requirement that board meetings be open to the members is inapplicable to meetings that are held for purposes of discussing personnel matters and meetings between the board and the association's attorney that are held for purposes of discussing pending or threatened litigation.[76]

---

70   §720.303 (2) (c) 2, F.S.
71   §720.303 (2) (b), F.S.
72   §720.303 (2) (d), F.S.
73   §720.303 (2) (d), F.S.
74   §720.303 (2) (b), F.S.
75   §720.306 (10), F.S.
76   §720.303 (2) (b), F.S.

3.12 Committees. The board of directors, in addition to selecting the officers of the homeowners association, may also designate an executive committee and other committees unless prohibited by the articles of incorporation or the bylaws.[77] The committees are created by resolution of the board of directors, and each committee exercising some authority of the board of directors must include two or more members of the board unless otherwise provided in the governing documents.[78]

Committees authorized to spend association funds, committees appointed to consider fines or suspensions,[79] or committees vested with the power to approve architectural decisions in the community must follow the same notice, quorum, and voting requirements imposed upon the board of directors of the association.[80] Meetings of these committees are open to members of the association, and committee members are not permitted to vote by proxy or by secret ballot.[81] (See 8.5.)

Committees authorized to consider fines, suspension of the rights to use the common areas, or suspension of a member's voting rights are specifically recognized and authorized by law. (See 13.7.) When appointing members of a committee to consider fines or suspension, however, the board may not appoint a current board member or an individual who resides in the household of a board member.[82]

Advisory committees also have a place within the organization of the homeowners association. They are not authorized by the community documents or by statute to carry out functions for the association or to exercise any authority on behalf of the board of directors.[83] Such advisory committees help analyze problems, review facts, and gather information and alternatives.

The conclusions and recommendations of advisory committees are reported to the board of directors or to the officer of the homeowners association creating the committee. As with other committees, the notice, quorum, and voting requirements imposed by statute should be followed by advisory committees to avoid questions concerning the use of or reliance on the committees' conclusions and recommendations by the board of directors.[84]

---

77   §617.0825 (1), F.S.
78   §617.0825 (3), F.S.
79   §720.305 (2) (b), F.S.
80   §720.303 (2) (a), F.S.
81   §720.303 (2) (c) 3, F.S.
82   §720.305 (2), F.S.
83   §617.0825 (1), F.S.
84   §720.303 (2) (c) 3, F.S.

4

Officers

4.1   General. The homeowners association can only carry out acts through its officers and agents. The board of directors makes the policies for the association, but the officers and agents carry out these policies and administrative functions for the community.[1]

Some of the officers are merely clerical or ministerial while others carry out substantive functions based on the policies established by the board. All of the officers of the homeowners association have a fiduciary relationship to the members of the association. (See 3.6.) The officers have an affirmative obligation to act with utmost good faith towards the association and cannot deal in the funds or the property of the association to their own advantage.[2]

Each homeowners association shall have such officers as are described in the articles of incorporation or bylaws. The officers shall serve for the terms prescribed in the association documents, and, if terms are not established, the officers shall be appointed by the board of directors annually.[3] The officers most commonly described by the association documents are a president, secretary, treasurer, and one or more vice presidents. Collectively, the officers will perform the duties established in the bylaws and carry out the management responsibilities of the homeowners association under the policies approved by the board of directors.[4]

4.2   Election of Officers. The officers of the homeowners association are elected, or appointed, by the board of directors. They are not elected by the membership of the association unless the bylaws of the association specifically require a membership vote for a particular office.[5] The officers are elected by a majority vote of the board of directors,[6] and the board is permitted to conduct the election for officers by secret ballot.[7] When the bylaws or the board of directors allows, any duly appointed or elected officer of the homeowners association may appoint one or more officers or assistant officers.[8] (See 4.8.)

4.3   President. The president of the homeowners association is traditionally vested with all the powers generally given to the chief

---

1   §617.0841, F.S.
2   §720.303 (1), F.S.
3   §617.0840 (1), F.S.
4   §617.0841, F.S.
5   §617.0840 (1), F.S.
6   §617.0824 (3), F.S.
7   §720.303 (2) (c) 3, F.S.
8   §617.0840 (2), F.S.

executive officer of a corporation.[9] While specific bylaw provisions may vary the president's duties, it is generally presumed that he or she will preside at all meetings of the board of directors and the membership.[10] The president will execute contracts approved by the board and other documents in the name of the association as its agent. When signing documents, the president should indicate the capacity in which he or she is signing to avoid any personal liability since the president's signature, under most circumstances, will bind the homeowners association under the doctrine of inherent powers.[11]

The president also assumes general charge of the day-to-day administration of the association and has the authority to authorize specific actions in furtherance of the board's policies. As chief executive officer, the president serves as spokesperson for the board of directors in most matters relating to general association business.[12] Like all officers of the association, the president has an affirmative duty to carry out the responsibilities of the office in the best interests of the association. The president serves at the will of the board of directors and can be removed with or without cause at any time by majority vote of the full board.[13]

The president cannot, without specific board approval, borrow funds in the name of the association or otherwise act beyond the scope of the authority established by the homeowners association documents and board of directors.[14] The president does have the inherent authority to appoint committees to advise him and to advise the board. The president also has the authority to appoint certain officers to assist him with his duties such as vote tellers, inspectors of elections, sergeants at arms, and a temporary secretary or recorder unless the bylaws otherwise make some provision for selection of these positions.[15]

4.4 Secretary. The bylaws or the board of directors are required to delegate to one of the officers responsibility for preparing notice for all meetings of the board and the membership and authenticating the records

9   *Pan-American Construction Co. v. Searcy*, 84 So.2d 540 (Fla. 1955); *18B Am. Jur. 2d, Corporations*, *§1534*.

10   *Robert's Rules of Order Newly Revised (1990)*, *§46*.

11   *Snead v. United States Trucking Corp.*, 380 So.2d 1075, 1078 (Fla. 1st DCA 1980); *Pan-American Construction Corp. v. Searcy, supra note 9.*

12   18B *Am. Jur. 2d, Corporations, §1534.*

13   *§617.0842 (2), F.S.; Frank v. Anthony*, 107 So.2d 136 (Fla. 2d DCA 1958).

14   See also *Lensa Corp. v. Poinciana Gardens Ass'n, Inc.*, 765 So.2d 296, 298 (Fla. 4'h DCA 2000) and *Wenger v. Breakwater Homeowners' Ass'n*, 423 So.2d 619 (Fla. 4th DCA 1982), *applying the general corporate law principle that a corporation's powers are limited to those expressed in the articles of incorporation and those implied powers necessary to perform the authorized functions of the association.*

15   18B *Am. Jur. 2d, Corporations, §1534; Fletcher's Cyclopedia on Corporations, Private Corporations*, *§533.*

of the association.[16] Customarily, such responsibilities are delegated to the secretary. The position of secretary is not simply a clerical position, however. In many cases, the secretary will not actually keep the minutes of the meetings but will be responsible for obtaining someone who will do so as a recorder or assistant secretary. As the custodian of the minutes and the other official records of the association, the secretary is responsible for ensuring access to those records by members and their authorized representatives.[17] (See 6.6.)

The homeowners association is authorized to adopt and use a "corporate seal."[18] When the secretary has been delegated the responsibility for authenticating records of the homeowners association, the verification customarily occurs by affixing the secretary's signature and placing the corporate seal on the appropriate document. By example, when the signature of the president binds the corporation, the secretary, as custodian of the seal, verifies the president's authority. The secretary does so by signing or attesting to the president's signature and placing the corporate seal on the appropriate document.[19]

4.5   Treasurer. The treasurer is traditionally the custodian of the funds, securities, and financial records of the association. When the association has a manager or other employee that actually handles the funds, then the treasurer's duties will include overseeing the appropriate employees to ensure that the financial records and reports are properly kept and maintained. Unless the bylaws otherwise specify, the treasurer is responsible for coordinating the development of the proposed annual budget and for preparing and giving the annual financial report.[20] (See 5.12.)

The treasurer does not have the authority to bind the association or the board of directors when dealing with third parties unless the board has provided express authority for the treasurer to do so.[21] As with the association's secretary, the treasurer does not have to actually perform the day-to-day record-keeping functions of the association, but the treasurer will ultimately be responsible to make sure that the financial records of the homeowners association have been maintained properly in accordance with good accounting practices.

---

16   §617.0840 (3), F.S.
17   §720.303 (3) and (4), F.S.
18   §617.0302 (3), F.S.; the seal must always contain the words "corporation not for profit." *Id.*
19   §617.0302 (3), F.S. and §692.01, F.S.
20   *Fletcher's Cyclopedia on Corporations, Private Corporations, §654; 18B Am. Jur. 2d, Corporations, §1538.*
21   *Ideal Foods, Inc. v. Action Leasing Corp., 413 So. 2d 416, 417 (Fla. 5th DCA 1982).*

4.6   Vice President. The vice president of the homeowners association is vested with all of the powers which are required to perform the duties of the association president in the absence of the president.[22] The vice president does not automatically possess inherent powers to act in the capacity of chief executive and may act for the president only when the president is actually absent or otherwise unable to act.[23] The vice president may assume such additional duties as are defined or assigned to the office by the board of directors of the association.[24]

In many communities, the vice president will be assigned specific areas of responsibility, which may include overseeing the care and maintenance of the grounds and buildings, the recreational properties, or other association properties. The vice president may also be designated to serve as the executive director or the employee manager for the association. Each of these duties must be specifically conveyed by the board of directors upon the vice president, and the scope of this authority and responsibility should be defined in writing and placed in the minutes or in the bylaws of the homeowners association.

4.7   Registered Agent and Office. The registered agent is a ministerial officer of the homeowners association, and it is an officer that is required of all corporations in Florida.[25] In addition to naming a registered agent, each homeowners association must also maintain a registered office for the corporation, although it does not need to be the same as the association's place of business.[26] The registered agent receives all formal service of legal papers on behalf of the association, including all lawsuits.

The registered agent is an important link for the homeowners association since many formal and important communications will be received by this association officer.[27] When these communications or documents are received, they must be brought immediately to the attention of the board of directors. The registered agent must be aware of the responsibilities of the office, and the board of directors may desire to assign this responsibility to a member of the current board or to the association's legal counsel.

---

22   18B *Am. Jur. 2d, Corporations, §1537; Fletcher's Cyclopedia on Corporations, Private Corporations,*
     §627.
23   *Pan-American Construction Co. v. Searcy, supra note 9; see also Robert's Rules of Order Newly Revised*
     (1990), §46.
24   §617.0841, F.S.
25   §617.0501 (1) (a), F.S.
26   §617.0501 (1) (b), F.S.
27   §607.0505, F.S.

The name of the registered agent and the street address of the registered office can be changed by the board of directors at any time by simply filing written notice with the Division of Corporations. The address for the registered office of the association must be a street address, and a post office box address is not acceptable. When the registered agent is changed, the new registered agent must sign the change in designation, acknowledging and accepting the responsibilities of the position.[28]

4.8 Other Officers. The homeowners association shall have such other officers as are provided for in the articles of incorporation, and such officers and assistant officers as may be authorized by the association bylaws or the board of directors.[29] Other officers may include an assistant secretary, additional vice presidents, or other positions which will serve merely as agents to carry out specific association responsibilities. These other officers will help divide the responsibilities of the association into manageable categories, and each office can be assigned specific authority by the board of directors to carry out the assigned duties and responsibilities.[30]

The responsibilities of supplemental association officers may include the authority to sign liens, demand letters, and checks for the association. They may include the authority to manage the day-to-day maintenance responsibilities for the association or other specific activities sanctioned by the board.[31] Custom allows third parties to rely on agents and officers of the association. A commitment made in the normal course of business by agents and officers may bind the association. (See 4.9.) When creating additional offices, the board should specify, in writing, the scope of authority for the office and the specific duties and responsibilities of the officer. The limits imposed upon the officer's authority should also be expressed.

4.9 Scope of Authority. The officers and agents of the homeowners association must carry out their duties within the scope of authority conferred upon the office.[32] The relationship between an officer and the association is that of principal and agent.[33] When the officer is acting on the homeowners association's behalf and within the scope of his or her

---

28   §617.0502, F.S.
29   §617.0840 (1) and (2), F.S.
30   §617.0841, F.S.
31   *Id.*
32   See *B & J Holding Corp. v. Miller, 353 So.2d 141, 143 (Fla. 3d DCA 1977).*
33   *Thomkin Corp. v. Miller, 24 So.2d 48 (Fla. 1945).*

authority, the association is bound by the acts of the officer or agent.[34] Individual association members or members of the public at large acting in good faith may rely on the "real" or "apparent" authority of an officer to bind the homeowners association.[35]

The "real" authority of an association officer is that which is expressly set out in the association's bylaws or in resolutions of the board of directors and which is actually known to the party dealing with the officer.[36] The "apparent" authority of an officer is grounded in the doctrine of estoppel.[37] It arises when the homeowners association allows or causes others to believe the officer has such authority through its actions or representations.[38] It may exist or arise from the very nature of the office itself.[39] Through an officer's authority, real or apparent, the association makes its financial commitments, enters into contracts for service, and otherwise carries on the business of the association.[40]

4.10 Resignation and Removal. Any officer of the homeowners association may resign at any time by delivering his or her written resignation to the association. The resignation is effective when the notice is delivered by the officer unless the notice specifies a later effective date. When the resignation is effective at a later date, the vacant office may be filled before the effective date of the resignation provided the successor does not take office until the vacancy is effective.[41]

An officer of the association may be removed by the board of directors at any time, with or without cause, by a majority vote at a properly called meeting of the board. An officer or assistant officer appointed by another officer may likewise be removed at any time with or without cause by the officer of the homeowners association who made the appointment.[42]

---

34 §617.0841, F.S.; see also *Stiles v. Gordon Land Co., 44 So.2d 417 (Fla. 1950) citing Thomkin Corp. v. Miller, supra note 33; see also Edward J. Gerrits, Inc. v. McKinney, 410 So.2d 542, 545 (Fla. 1ˢt DCA 1982).*

35 *Id.*

36 18 B. *Am. Jur. 2d, Corporations, §1521.*

37 "Its (the doctrine of estoppel) three primary elements are: (1) representation by the principal, (2) reliance upon that representation by a third person, and (3) a change of position by the third person in reliance upon such representation." *Ideal Foods, Inc. v. Action Leasing Corp., 413 So.2d 416, 418 (Fla. 5th DCA 1982) citing Stiles v. Gordon Land Co., supra note 34.*

38 *Taco Bell of California v. Zappone, 324 So.2d 121, 123–124 (Fla. 2d DCA 1975).*

39 *Pan-American Construction Co. v. Searcy, supra note 9.*

40 *Dade County Dairies, Inc. v. Projected Planning Co., 158 So.2d 565 (Fla. 3d DCA 1963); see also 18B Am. Jur. 2d, Corporations, §1519 and §1521.*

41 §617.0842 (1), F.S.

42 §617.0842 (2), F.S.

4.11 Compensation. Unless the community's governing documents authorize a fee or salary,[43] or unless a salary or other compensation is approved in advance by a majority of the voting interests in the homeowners association,[44] the officers and directors may not be paid for their service. These officials are required to perform their duties on behalf of the association without any fee or salary, and they may not benefit financially from their service to the association in any other way.[45]

Although compensation is not permitted for officers and directors, individuals serving in these capacities may receive financial benefits accruing to other members of the homeowners association from the maintenance, repair, and replacement of the association property[46] and from the recovery of insurance proceeds from policies maintained by the association for the benefit of the membership.[47] Officers and directors are also entitled to reimbursement for out-of-pocket expenses incurred on behalf of the homeowners association.[48]

---

43   §720.303 (12) (d), F.S.
44   §720.303 (12) (e), F.S.
45   §720.303 (12), F.S. The salary and compensation restrictions also apply to committee members.
46   §720.303 (12) (a), F.S.
47   §720.303 (12) (c), F.S.
48   §720.303 (12) (b), F.S.

5
Budget and Finances

5.1   General. Each homeowners association is required to keep its financial records according to generally accepted accounting principles.[1] Key among these financial records is the financial plan that sets forth the proposed expenditure of funds for the maintenance of the properties under the association's control and for the management and operation of the association itself. The financial plan, or budget, is the foundation document for the association's financial operation and stability. It provides a preview of the coming year's expenses, and it provides a benchmark by which the previous year's expenditures can be judged and evaluated.

The budget must be prepared annually by the community for a twelve-month period.[2] Once adopted, it becomes the basis for allocating the individual assessment shares among each of the members of the homeowners association. The manner for allocating shares among the members of the association will be established by the community documents. Upon adoption of the budget, the required annual assessment or amenity fee of each parcel owner in the community is also simultaneously set, and the owner becomes obligated to pay the association the sums due for the operation of the community.[3] Notice of any meeting of the board of directors in which assessments against parcels are to be established, including assessments to fund the annual budget, must be specially prepared to advise parcel owners concerning the nature of the assessments.[4] (See 5.6.)

5.2   Recurring Operations. The budget for the homeowners association must provide an accurate, itemized, and detailed listing of all the expenses that the community reasonably believes will be incurred during the coming fiscal year. The main categories or components of the budget will govern the regular and ongoing operations of the homeowners association. These operations categories will deal with the everyday, recurring expenditures of the community, and they should identify each proposed category of expense separately, from administration to management, and from taxes to insurance.[5]

The expenses for general operations should be listed by account and classification, and they should be set out to show the total estimated monthly and annual expenditures for each classification. It is helpful to have the categories coded with a numbering system or other identifying

---

1   §720.303 (4) (j), F.S.
2   §720.303 (8), F.S.
3   §720.301 (11) (b), F.S.
4   §720.303 (2) (c) 2, F.S.
5   §720.303 (6), F.S.; *Berg v. Bridle Path Homeowners Ass'n, Inc., 809 So.2d 32, 33 (Fla. 4th DCA 2002).*

subtitle so that actual expenditures through the course of the fiscal year can be allocated to the appropriate category or account.

5.3 Reserves for Deferred Maintenance.

In many communities, it is prudent to have a separate portion of the budget set aside that creates reserve accounts for capital expenditures and deferred maintenance.[6] These budget reserves are intended to fund items of expense that do not occur on a regular basis, and their purpose is to provide for the longer-term needs of the homeowners association which involve major capital repairs or replacements to the property of the association. The reserve categories may include funds for roadways and repaving or for capital repairs to the community recreation building and other types of shared facilities.

Reserve accounts in many communities are required by law, and the accounts become a mandatory component of the community's budget if the reserves are initially provided for by the developer or when a majority of the voting interests in the association have elected to provide for reserve accounts.[7] Once an association provides for reserve accounts, the reserve funds must be budgeted, maintained, and waived as the law requires.[8] When the association is not required to reserve, it must disclose that the association budget does not include reserve accounts in conspicuous type on the annual financial report of the association.[9] When the budget provides for only limited voluntary reserves, a similar disclosure statement must appear in conspicuous type in the annual financial report for the accounting period.[10] (See 5.12.)

The amount of reserves for each budget category must computed by means of a formula that will take into consideration the estimated useful life of the asset and the amount of money that will be required to make the repair or replacement when it is actually needed.[11] The law does permit "pooled" reserve accounts that include two or more capital assets of the association, and the formula for calculating the pooled reserves must reflect the remaining useful life and estimated replacement cost for each asset included in the pooled account.[12] The basis or formula for establishing the reserve amounts should be stated as a part of the budget as

---

6   §720.303 (6) (b), F.S.
7   §720.303 (6) (d), F.S. The majority approval may be attained by vote at a duly called meeting or by written consent. Once approved, the requirement may be later terminated by majority approval.
8   §720.303 (6) (b), F.S.
9   §720.303 (6) (c) 1., F.S.
10   *Id.*
11   §720.303 (6) (e) and (g), F.S.
12   §720.303 (6) (g), F.S.

a footnote so the information will be available for review by members of the association.[13]

The reserve funds maintained by the homeowners association may be jointly invested with the operating monies of the association, but the jointly invested funds must be accounted for separately in the financial records of the association.[14]

5.4   Waiver of Mandatory Reserves.

When the homeowners association establishes reserve accounts, the members of the community may waive the collection of reserves for a specific budget year or provide for the collection of less reserves than are otherwise required by the statutory formula. To authorize the waiver or to provide for less reserves than required, the action must be approved by a majority vote of the membership at a duly called meeting at which a quorum is present.[15]

Once reserve funds have been collected, the funds and any accruing interest on them must remain in the designated accounts and used only for authorized reserve expenditures unless the membership of the association approves their use for other purposes. To use the funds in a designated reserve account for another purpose, the expenditure must be approved, in advance of the expenditure, by a majority vote of the association membership at a duly called meeting at which a quorum is present.[16]

5.5   Recreational Amenities.

The recreational amenities serving the community may be available through membership arrangements or other agreements (see 6.9), or the recreation properties may be owned by the association, the developer, or another person. Notwithstanding their ownership, however, special treatment of the fees and charges for the recreational amenities is required under the law governing homeowners associations. The budget for the association is required to set out separately all fees and charges for recreational amenities no matter who retains ownership of the property.[17] In corresponding fashion, the annual financial report to the members must set out the actual receipts and expenditures for the recreational amenities.[18]

When parcel owners are required to pay maintenance or amenity fees directly to the developer or to another owner of recreational facilities

---

13   §720.303 (6) (g), F.S. The financial records of the association must be kept according to good accounting practices. §720.303 (4) (j), F.S.

14   §720.303 (8) (a), F.S.

15   §720.303 (6) (f), F.S.

16   §720.303 (6) (h), F.S.

17   §720.303 (6) (a), F.S.

18   §720.303 (7) (b), F.S.

or other properties, the owner of the facilities is required to provide a complete financial report of the actual, total receipts of the fees received from the parcel owners.[19] The report must be provided within sixty (60) days following the end of each fiscal year, and it may be given by mail to each parcel owner, by publishing it in a publication regularly distributed within the community or by posting it in prominent locations within the community.[20]

5.6   Developing the Proposed Budget. The "proposed budget" is the preliminary draft of the homeowners association's financial plan, and it is offered by the board or other association officer for formal adoption as the budget. The development of the proposed budget may be by the association's treasurer, a financial committee, the community's management company, or by the board of directors itself.

The board should bring as much expertise as possible to the development of the proposed budget. The records of each homeowners association must include an accurate record of previous expenditures so that the proposed budget can be based on the association's financial history and the experience of the previous year's expenditures.[21] New anticipated expenses can be estimated from comparisons in the marketplace or from the experience of other homeowners associations. Each classification should be based upon realistic estimates and should be set forth in sufficient detail so that each category can be understood and evaluated by the members of the association and by the board of directors.

The proposed budget must contain the reserve accounts with the projection for full funding of the capital expenditures and deferred maintenance requirements when reserves are mandatory.[22] (See 5.3.) The proposed budget cannot anticipate that reserves will be waived by the members or that the members will provide for reserves in an amount less than is adequate. During the formal adoption procedures, the proposed budget becomes the actual budget, but only a proper vote by the membership may remove or modify the reserve provisions from the proposed budget.[23] (See 5.4.)

5.7   Funding the Budget. To fund the homeowners association's budget, the board of directors, in almost all circumstances, is granted

---

19   Any amounts paid to the homeowners association, to local governmental entities, and special taxing
        districts do not need to be included in the report. §689.265, F.S.
20   §689.265, F.S.
21   See §720.303 (4) (j) 1. and 3., F.S.
22   §720.303 (6) (f), F.S.
23   *Id.*

authority to assess individual property owners for their share of the community's funding requirements.[24] The recorded declaration of covenants and the other governing documents of the association must be consulted to determine the basis for the assessment allocation.[25] The assessments must be allocated based upon the members' proportional shares as described in the governing documents, and it is permissible for the documents to provide for different shares among classes of parcel owners.[26]

In the unlikely event that no specific allocation is made in the community's documents, then the responsibility for funding the budget should be spread equally among the parcels of property represented in the homeowners association. For communities created after October 1, 1995, the governing documents are required to describe the manner in which expenses are shared by the members, and the documents must specify the proportional shares for which each member is responsible.[27]

Notice of the board of directors meeting where assessments are to be established must contain a specific statement that assessments will be considered and a statement concerning the nature of the assessments. The meeting notice must be mailed, delivered, or electronically transmitted to each member of the homeowners association and posted in a conspicuous place on the association property at least fourteen (14) days before the meeting.[28] (See 3.10.)

When the amount of the annual assessment has been determined for each member, the board of directors is then required to establish a payment schedule for the owners. In many cases, the payment schedule will be described the bylaws or in the covenants governing the association. If a schedule is not established by the community documents, the board must, by resolution, determine whether the assessment will be paid in full or be divided into monthly or quarterly installments. The board of directors should require that payments be made in advance so that the funds are available to meet the current needs of the association as they arise.[29] When the annual budget has been approved, the board of directors must provide each member with a copy of the budget or written notice that a copy of the budget is available upon request at no charge to the member.[30] The association must maintain a current account and a periodic statement of

---

24   §720.301 (1), F.S.; see *Wood v. McElvey, 296 So.2d 102 (Fla. 2d DCA 1974)*.
25   See *Bessemer v. Gersten, 381 So.2d 1344 (Fla. 1980)*.
26   §720.308 (1), F.S.
27   *Id.*
28   §720.303 (2) (b) 2, F.S.
29   §720.303 (6) (a), F.S. and § 720.308 (1) (a), F.S.
30   §720.303 (6), F.S.

the account, designating the name of the member, the due date and amount of each assessment, the amount paid upon the account, and the balance due from each member of the homeowners association.[31] The association must also maintain insurance or a fidelity bond for all persons who control and disburse the funds of the association in an amount sufficient to cover the maximum funds in the custody of the association.[32] (See 3.7.)

5.8   Time for Payment and Delinquency. The timely remittance of assessments and assessment installments from each member is essential to the smooth functioning of the homeowners association and the proper maintenance of the community's property. A parcel owner is liable for all assessments that come due while he or she is the owner of the parcel, and the obligation for the assessments may not be avoided by waiver or suspension of the use of the common property.[33] A parcel owner is jointly and severally liable with the previous owner for all unpaid assessments or assessment installments that came due prior to the time of transfer of title to the parcel.[34]

When exercising its authority to set the assessment levels, the board of directors must appropriately establish specific due dates for the assessment or the assessment installments. In addition to a due date, the board should also identify the point in time when the payment becomes delinquent.[35] The payment procedures should be contained in a resolution or in the minutes of the board of directors meeting. They should also be included in the assessment notices which are provided to each member of the association. The clarity of the board of directors' actions and the responsibility of each member of the association is an essential ingredient to ensure timely payment by responsible members and to ensure effective enforcement against delinquent members.

Assessments and installments on an assessment that are not paid when due bear interest from the due date until paid at the rate provided in the governing documents, and if the documents permit, an administrative late fee may also be charged in an amount that does not exceed the greater of $25.00 or five (5) percent of the past-due sums. Delinquency by an owner may also result in the loss of privileges to use the common areas in the community. (See 5.10.) Any payment received by the association

---

31   §720.303 (4) (j) 2., F.S.
32   §720.3033 (5), F.S.
33   §720.3085 (1), F.S.
34   §720.3085 (2), F.S.
35   §720.303 (4) (j) 2., F.S.

from a delinquent owner is applied first to any interest accrued, then to any costs incurred in collection, and then to the delinquent assessment.[36]

5.9   Enforcement and Liens. The association, through its board of directors, has the power to both establish and collect the assessments.[37] The enforcement rights that the association has against delinquent members include the right to lien the delinquent parcel owner.[38] Prior to filing a lien, however, the board of directors must make written demand for the unpaid amounts by registered or certified mail and provide the owner with forty-five (45) days to remit all amounts due to the association.[39]

If the parcel owner remains delinquent after the expiration of the 45-day period, the homeowners association may proceed to lien the parcel. When exercising the lien rights provided to the association, the board of directors should evidence its claim by filing a formal "claim of lien" with the appropriate recording officer in the county where the property is located. The claim of lien becomes effective on the date of its recording and continues until the assessment, late fees, and the costs of collection are paid in full.[40]

The priority of the lien is determined by the declaration of covenants.[41] When the declaration provides, the lien of the first mortgagee will take precedence over the association's claim of lien. Alternatively, if the declaration permits, the lien of the homeowners association for delinquent assessments may take priority over the mortgage of a parcel owner.[42]

The claim of lien should state the legal description of the property, the name of the property owner, and the amount and date when the assessment or assessment installment became due. The claim of lien should be signed by an officer or agent of the homeowners association. Once it has been recorded, the association may be bring an action to foreclose the lien and collect the unpaid amounts provided that an

---

36   §720.3085 (3), F.S.

37   §720.301 (1), §720.303 (6), and §720.3085, F.S.

38   §720.301 (1) and (11) (b), F.S.; see also *Bessemer v. Gersten, supra at note 25.*

39   §720.3085 (4), F.S.

40   Pursuant to §95.11(2)(b), F.S., unless the governing documents provide for another time frame, the lien must be foreclosed within 5 years or the claim is barred by the statute of limitations.

41   *Ecoventure WGV, Ltd. V. Saint Johns Northwest Residential Ass'n, Inc., 56 So.3d 126 (Fla. 5th DCA 2011); Coral Lakes Community Ass'n, Inc. v. Busey Bank, 30 So.3d 579, 584 (Fla. 2d DCA 2010).*

42   *Holly Lake Ass'n v. Federal National Mortgage Ass'n, 660 So.2d 266 (Fla. 1995) citing New York Life Insurance & Annuity Corp. v. Hammocks Community Assoc., 622 So.2d 1369 (Fla. 3d DCA 1993). The superiority in lien rights relies on specific language in the declaration. See Ass'n of Poinciana Villages v. Avatar Properties, Inc., 724 So.2d 585 (Fla. 5th DCA 1998) and Federal National Mortgage Ass'n v. McKesson, 639 So.2d 78 (Fla. 4th DCA 1994).*

additional 45-day written notice has been given to the parcel owner of the association's intent to foreclose.[43]

At any time during the pendency of formal foreclosure proceedings, the delinquent parcel owner may serve a "qualifying offer" with the court and the association's attorney and stay the proceedings. The qualifying offer must be notarized and in writing, and it must promise to pay all sums due the association within sixty (60) days.[44] If the sums are not paid within sixty (60) days or if the delinquent owner does not abide by the terms of the qualifying offer, the foreclosure proceedings may proceed to a final judgment in favor of the association.[45] When the association acquires title to a lot or parcel through foreclosure, it is not liable for delinquent assessments due to any other association.[46]

When an owner is delinquent in his or her financial obligation to the homeowners association, the remaining association members assume an unfair share of the community's financial responsibilities. As a result, the board of directors should not be reluctant to use the collection sanctions which the community documents allow.

5.10 Suspension of Rights. In addition to its lien rights, the homeowners association has other available sanctions that it may impose against delinquent parcel owners. The law permits fines and the suspension of a member's rights to use the common areas in the community when the owner is more than ninety (90) days past due in any monetary obligation due to the association.[47] However, the suspension of rights to use and access the common properties cannot extend to vehicular and pedestrian ingress and egress to the lot or parcel of the owner.[48] The association may also suspend the voting rights of a member for the nonpayment of regular annual assessments that are delinquent for more than ninety (90) days, and the suspension ends upon full payment of all obligations currently due or overdue to the association.[49]

Any proposed fine or suspension against a parcel owner must be preceded by at least fourteen (14) days' notice, and the delinquent owner must be given the opportunity for a hearing on the proposed sanctions. The notice from the homeowners association must be in writing and must be provided by mail or by hand delivery. The hearing will be before a

---

43 §720.3085 (4), F.S.
44 §720.3085 (6) (b) and (c), F.S.
45 §720.3085 (6) (d), F.S.
46 §720.3085 (2) (d), F.S.
47 §720.305 (2) (b), F.S.
48 §720.305 (3), F.S.
49 §720.305 (4), F.S.

committee of at least three (3) individuals who are independent of the board of directors, and if the committee does not approve the fine or suspension by a majority vote, the sanction cannot be imposed.[50] (See 7.5.)

5.11 Collection of Delinquencies from Tenant.

If a home is occupied by a tenant and the owner is delinquent in assessment obligations due to the homeowners association, the association may collect the delinquent obligations from the monies the tenant is obligated to pay the homeowner after serving the tenant with written demand for payment by the required statutory notice.[51] A copy of the notice for payment must also be provided to the parcel owner.[52] The tenant, acting in good faith and paying sums to the association in lieu of the owner, is entitled to full credit for the payments and is immune to any claim by the parcel owner for the payments made to the association.[53] The association must appropriately account for the funds received, and upon request, it must provide written receipts to the tenant for the sums paid by the tenant.[54]

If the tenant fails to pay the association after the written demand has been properly made, the association may proceed with eviction proceedings against the tenant as if it were the landlord.[55] The tenant is not obligated for increases in amounts due to the association unless written notice of the increase has been made at least ten (10) days before the date that the rent is due to the owner. A court may supersede the effect of the demand for payment to the association by appointing a receiver.[56]

5.12 Annual Financial Report.

Each year the board of directors must provide, by mail or personal delivery to all members, a copy of the association's annual financial report or a written notice that a copy of the report is available upon request at no charge to the member.[57] The financial report must consist of financial statements presented in conformity with generally accepted accounting principles based upon the total annual revenue of the association.[58]

The board of directors is required to prepare the appropriate annual

---

50   §720.305 (2) (b), F.S.; see also *Tahiti Beach Homeowners Ass'n v. Pfeffer, 52 So.3d 808 (Fla. 3d DCA 2011).*

51   §720.3085 (8), F.S.

52   §720.3085 (8) (a), F.S.

53   §720.3085 (8) (b), F.S. The tenant does not have any rights to vote or inspect the association records by virtue of the payments made to the association.

54   §720.3085 (8) (a), F.S.

55   §720.3085 (8) (c), F.S.

56   §720.3085 (8) (e), F.S.

57   *Romero v. Shadywood Villas Homeowners Association, Inc. 657 So.2d 1193 (Fla. 3d DCA 1995).*

58   §720.303 (7) (a), F.S.

financial report within ninety (90) days after the close of the fiscal year of the association,[59] and the board must provide the report or the required notice of its availability to the members of the homeowners association within twenty-one (21) days of its completion.[60]

An association with total annual revenues between $150,000 and $300,000 is required to prepare compiled financial statements. An association with total annual revenues between $300,000 and $500,000 is required to prepare reviewed financial statements, and an association with total annual revenues of $500,000 or more is required to prepare audited financial statements.[61] Associations that have annual revenues of less than $150,000 are only required to prepare a report of cash receipts and expenditures, and an association of fewer than fifty (50) parcels may prepare a report consisting of only cash receipts and expenditures, regardless of the annual revenues, unless the governing documents of the association require otherwise.[62]

By petition, twenty (20) percent of the association membership may require the board of directors to call a special meeting of the membership to consider a higher level of financial reporting than the minimum level of reporting required by law. Within thirty (30) days of receipt of the petition, the board of directors is required to notice and hold a membership meeting to consider the petition. If the higher level of reporting is approved by a majority of the total voting interests of the association, the board shall make the necessary funds available for the modified financial report, and the report shall be completed and available within ninety (90) days.[63]

The association membership may also provide for a lower level of reporting upon a majority vote of the members present at a properly called membership meeting, but the association must, at a minimum, provide a report of the cash receipts and expenditures.[64] The report of the cash receipts and expenditures is required to disclose the amounts of all receipts by account and classification, as well as the amount of expenditures by account and classification.[65] When the association is responsible for repair and maintenance of capital improvements and the budget is not required to provide for statutory reserve accounts, each annual financial report shall contain the following statement in conspicuous type:[66]

---

59   *Id.*
60   The report must be available within 21 days of its completion, but not later than 120 days after the close of the fiscal year. §720.303 (7), F.S.
61   §720.303 (7) (a), F.S.
62   §720.303 (7) (b), F.S.
63   §720.303 (7) (c), F.S.
64   §720.303 (7) (d), F.S.
65   §720.303 (7) (b) 3, F.S.
66   §720.303 (6) (c) 1., F.S.

THE BUDGET OF THE ASSOCIATION DOES NOT PROVIDE FOR RESERVE ACCOUNTS FOR CAPITAL EXPENDITURES AND DEFERRED MAINTENANCE THAT MAY RESULT IN SPECIAL ASSESSMENTS. OWNERS MAY ELECT TO PROVIDE FOR RESERVE ACCOUNTS PURSUANT TO SECTION 720.303 (6), FLORIDA STATUTES, UPON OBTAINING APPROVAL OF NOT LESS THAN A MAJORITY OF THE TOTAL VOTING INTERESTS OF THE ASSOCIATION BY VOTE OF THE MEMBERS AT A MEETING OR BY WRITTEN CONSENT.

If the budget for the preceding year provides for reserves, but the reserves are not established by the members pursuant to the statute, the annual financial report must contain the following statement in conspicuous type:[67]

THE BUDGET OF THE ASSOCIATION PROVIDES FOR LIMITED VOLUNTARY DEFERRED EXPENDITURE ACCOUNTS, INCLUDING CAPITAL EXPENDITURES AND DEFERRED MAINTENANCE, SUBJECT TO LIMITS ON FUNDING CONTAINED IN OUR GOVERNING DOCUMENTS. BECAUSE THE OWNERS HAVE NOT ELECTED TO PROVIDE FOR RESERVE ACCOUNTS PURSUANT TO SECTION 720.303 (6), FLORIDA STATUTES, THESE FUNDS ARE NOT SUBJECT TO THE RESTRICTIONS ON USE OF SUCH FUNDS SET FORTH IN THAT STATUTE, NOR ARE RESERVES CALCULATED IN ACCORDANCE WITH THAT STATUTE.

5.13 Annual Financial Filings. In addition to the annual financial report, two additional financial filings are required annually of Florida homeowners associations. Each homeowners association, whether organized for profit or not-for-profit, is required to file an annual corporate report with Florida's Division of Corporations.[68] The annual report must be filed between January 1st and July 1st of each year, and it is required to maintain the association in an active status and in good standing under Florida corporate law. The report is filed on Division forms and must set forth the corporate name, the address of the principle office, the corporation's federal tax identification number, and the name and the mailing address of each officer and director effective as of December

---

67   *Id.*
68   §617.1622, F.S.

31st of the year immediately preceding the due date of the report. The annual report must be accompanied by an annual filing fee payable to the Division.

Each association is also required to file an annual income tax return with the Internal Revenue Service.[69] A corporation organized not-for-profit is neither tax exempt nor exempt from filing an annual tax return. The Internal Revenue Service allows homeowners associations special treatment for some of their activities, including the retention of reserve accounts, but proper accounting for these funds and the filing of an income tax return are annual requirements for each community.

5.14 Contracts for Products and Services.
Any contract for the purchase or lease of materials or equipment that cannot be performed within one (1) year and all contracts for the provision of services to the homeowners association are required to be in writing. Additionally, any contract for materials or equipment or for the provision of services that requires payments by the association that exceed ten (10) percent of the total annual budget of the association, including reserves, must be competitively bid by the board of directors.[70]

The board is not required to accept the lowest bid,[71] and competitive bidding requirements do not limit the association's ability to obtain needed products and services in an emergency.[72] An association whose governing documents specifically provide for competitive bidding will govern the bidding process, provided that the document requirements are not less stringent than the requirements of the law.[73] All bids received by the homeowners association are considered official records of the association and must be kept for a period of at least one (1) year.[74]

Contracts with employees of the homeowners association, and contracts for the services of an attorney, accountant, architect, community manager, engineer, or a landscape architect, are not required to be competitively bid by the association. When a contract with a manager is competitively bid, however, it may be made for a period of up to three (3) years in length.[75] Contracts for materials and services provided to the association under a local government franchise agreement by the franchise

---

69   The tax returns of the homeowners' association are part of the financial and accounting records of the
       association. §720.303 (4) (j) 3, F.S.
70   §720.3055 (1), F.S.
71   *Id.*
72   §720.3055 (2) (b), F.S.
73   §720.3055 (2) (a), F.S.
74   §720.303 (4) (i), F.S.
75   §720.3055 (2) (a), F.S.

holder, renewal of contracts competitively bid that provide the board may cancel on thirty (30) days' notice,[76] and sole source contracts[77] are exempt from competitive bidding requirements.

If the association enters into a contract with one or more of its directors or a firm in which an officer or director has a financial interest, appropriate disclosure of the financial interest must be made;[78] the contract must be approved by at least two-thirds of the directors present; and the disclosure must be entered into the minutes of the meeting where the contract was approved.[79] The financial interest must also be disclosed at the next regular or special meeting of the membership, and upon a motion by any member, the contract may be canceled upon a majority vote of the members present.[80]

---

76   *Id.*
77   §720.3055 (2) (c), F.S.
78   §617.0832, F.S.
79   §720.3033 (2) (a)-(c), F.S.
80   §720.3033 (2) (d), F.S.

6

Rights and Responsibilities of the Parcel Owner

6.1   General. The declaration of covenants and the other governing documents of the community are for the collective benefit of the members of the homeowners association. They establish the tenor for the community, and they define the rights and responsibilities of the individual association members. The laws governing Florida homeowners associations are intended to support the community concept established by the governing documents while protecting the rights of the individual parcel owners.[1]

Each parcel owner is presumed to have knowledge of the community's governing documents,[2] and occupancy of the property in the community by a parcel owner must be consistent with the community concept. Under the law and the declaration of covenants, the owner of a parcel enjoys numerous rights and benefits. They may vary significantly based upon the language of an individual community's documents, but each owner is entitled to rely upon the content of the governing documents and the benefits conferred in them concerning the use of property in the community. These rights and benefits are appurtenances to the ownership of a parcel and run with the land.[3]

6.2   Use of the Common Area. The right to use the easements, common areas, and recreational amenities in accordance with the purposes for which they are intended is an appurtenance guaranteed to each parcel owner.[4] The rights of parcel owners and their visitors and guests to use the common areas, however, may not hinder nor unreasonably encroach upon the lawful rights of other parcel owners. By example, speed bumps placed on a private road by a homeowners association have been determined to substantially diminish the rights of individual owners to use the road and, therefore, constitute an improper or unreasonable restriction on the use of the common area.[5] Similarly, a dock constructed on association-owned property for the benefit of a single parcel owner was also deemed to violate the rights of the other owners entitled to the use and benefit of the common property.[6]

The right of a parcel owner to use the common areas includes the

1   §720.302 (1), F.S.

2   *Eastpointe Prop. Owners' Ass'n v. Cohen, 504 So.2d 518 (Fla. 4th DCA 1987), citing Hidden Harbour Estates v. Basso, 393 So.2d 637 (Fla. 4th DCA 1981).*

3   See generally, *Hagan v. Sabal Palms, Inc., 186 So.2d 302 (Fla. 2d DCA 1966); Black's Law Dictionary, 5th Ed. Rev.*

4   §720.301 (2) and §720.304 (1), F.S.; see also *S & T Anchorage, Inc. v. Lewis, 575 So.2d 696 (Fla. 3d DCA 1991).*

5   *Monell v. Golfview Road Ass'n, 359 So.2d 2 (Fla. 4th DCA 1978) and Normandy B. Condominium Ass'n, Inc. v. Normandy C. Condominium Ass'n, Inc., 541 So.2d 1263 (Fla. 4th DCA 1989).*

6   *Johnson v. Tlush, 468 So.2d 1023 (Fla. 4th DCA 1985).*

right to peaceably assemble in the common facilities and the right to invite public officers or candidates for public office to appear and speak on the common facilities.[7] Any parcel owner prevented from exercising the rights guaranteed by the law for use of the common areas or recreational facilities for their intended purposes may bring a civil action to enforce the rights guaranteed parcel owners if mediation of the dispute is unsuccessful.[8] (See 7.4.)

The rights of a parcel owner to use common areas and facilities may be denied for a reasonable period of time if the governing documents of the homeowners association authorize the suspension of these rights for violations of the community's covenants and restrictions.[9] (See 7.5.) Rights of an owner to use the common facilities may also be suspended for delinquent assessments when the governing documents permit.[10] (See 5.10.) The suspension of use rights to the common areas may not, however, impair the right of a parcel owner or the tenant of a parcel to have vehicular and pedestrian ingress and egress to and from the parcel, including the right to park an authorized motor vehicle.[11]

6.3   Guests and Tenants of a Parcel Owner.
The guests and tenants of a member of the association are covered by the provisions of the governing documents for the community and the law governing homeowners associations in Florida.[12] As such, they enjoy the rights to use and occupy the common areas and property in the community in the manner authorized by the documents.[13] When an owner is more than 90 days delinquent in monetary obligations due to the association, however, the privileges of a guest or tenant to use the common areas and facilities may be suspended until the owner's obligation has been paid.[14] (See 5.10.)

Guests and tenants are also required to comply with the covenants, restrictions, and rules of the association governing the use of the properties in the community.[15] The failure of a guest or tenant to comply with the community's governing documents subjects the individual parcel owner to possible mediation proceedings, court action, and other sanctions for any violation that is committed by a guest or tenant.[16] (See 7.4 and 7.5.)

---

7   §720.304 (1), F.S.

8   §720.305 (1), F.S.; see also *Lewis v. S & T Anchorage, Inc., 616 So.2d 478 (Fla. 3d DCA 1993).*

9   §720.305 (2), F.S.

10   §720.305 (2) (b), F.S.

11   §720.305 (2) (c), F.S.

12   §720.302 (1), F.S.

13   §720.304 (1) (c), F.S.

14   §720.305 (3), F.S.

15   §720.305 (1), F.S.

16   §720.305 (1) (d) and (2), F.S.

6.4 Membership and Voting Rights in the Association.

Every parcel owner or the owner's agent is entitled to membership in the homeowners association designated by the declaration of covenants as the managing entity for the community.[17] Each association member is distributed a voting interest by the governing documents as an appurtenance to membership in the homeowners association,[18] and the voting rights of a member may not be suspended by the association unless specifically authorized by the governing documents for the nonpayment of regular annual assessments.[19] (See 5.10.) Unless the governing documents provide otherwise, membership in the association extends to each owner of a parcel having multiple owners.

Members of the homeowners association have all of the voting rights granted them by the governing documents for the community.[20] Additionally, as a member of the association, there are certain related rights and privileges guaranteed to each member by statute. Association members are eligible to be nominated to, and serve as a member of, the board of directors of the homeowners association.[21] Members are entitled to receive prior notice of all meetings of the board of directors[22] and the membership.[23] Copies of the association budget and the annual financial report are available to all members at no charge,[24] and the records of the association are available for inspection by members at reasonable times and places.[25] (See 6.6.)

6.5 Participation in Association Affairs. No member of the

homeowners association may act on behalf of the association simply by reason of being a member,[26] but each member has the right to participate in important parts of the association's decision-making processes. All members have the right to attend and participate in all meetings of the membership and to exercise their voting interest, either in person or by proxy, on any and all decisions made at such meetings, including the selection of directors for the association.[27] When the homeowners

---

17   §720.301 (9) and (10), F.S.
18   §720.301 (13), F.S.; see also *Villages at Mango Key v. Hunter Development, Inc., 763 So.2d 476 (Fla. 5th DCA 2000).*
19   §720.305 (2) (d), F.S.
20   §720.301 (4), F.S.
21   §720.306 (9), F.S.
22   §720.303 (2), F.S.
23   §720.306 (4), F.S.
24   §720.303 (8) and (9), F.S.
25   §720.303 (5), F.S.
26   §720.303 (1), F.S.; see also §617.0604 (1), F.S.
27   §720.306 (2), (6), and (7), F.S.

association fails to fill enough vacancies on the board to constitute a quorum, it is the right of any member to petition the circuit court for the appointment of a receiver to look after the affairs of the association until a quorum can be attained.[28] (See 3.3.)

Any member of the association is authorized by law to tape-record or videotape any meetings of the association membership, as well as meetings of the board of directors. The right to record such meetings may be subject to reasonable restrictions provided that the restrictions have been adopted in advance by the board of directors.[29] Members also have the right under the law to place items before the board of directors and to speak on items when they appear on the agenda of the board meeting.[30] (See 3.11.)

The rights and privileges granted by the governing documents are for the benefit of the community and each member of the community. No amendments may be made to the governing documents unless they are first presented to the members of the association for their approval in accordance with the requirements stated in the documents. If no threshold of approval is stated in the documents, an affirmative vote of two-thirds of the voting interests in the association is required.[31] When an amendment affects vested rights of parcel owners, all owners affected by the change and all affected lien holders must join in the execution of the amendments to the documents.[32] (See 7.10.)

6.6 Access to Association Records. Most of the records of a homeowners association are available to the association members. Before a prospective purchaser becomes a parcel owner and member of the homeowners association, the purchaser must be presented a disclosure summary of the community's governing documents.[33] Upon request, the association is required to provide a complete copy of the recorded governing documents to any association member or prospective purchaser who requests them. The association may charge for the actual costs for reproducing and furnishing the documents to those persons entitled to receive them.[34] (See 6.8.)

---

28   §720.305 (3), F.S.; see also *Metro-Dade Investments, Co. v. Granada Lakes Villas Condominium, Inc., 74 So3d 593, 594 (Fla. 2d DCA 2011).*

29   §720.306 (10), F.S.

30   §720.303 (2) (b) and (d), F.S.

31   §720.306 (1) (b), F.S.

32   §720.306(1)(b) and (c), F.S.; *Palma v. Townhouses of Oriole Ass'n, Inc., 610 So.2d 112 (Fla. 4th DCA 1992); see also Norwood-Norland Homeowners v. Dade County, 511 So.2d 1009, 1014 (Fla. 3d DCA 1987).*

33   §720.401 (1) (a), F.S.

34   §720.303 (5) (c), F.S.

The other official records of the homeowners association are also open to inspection and available for photocopying by members of the association or their authorized representatives, and all of the official records of the association must be maintained within the state of Florida and be available within forty-five (45) miles of the community or within the county where the condominium is located.[35] If the association has a copy machine available, it must provide the copies upon request during the inspection if the request is limited to no more than twenty-five (25) pages, and the association may charge up to twenty-five (25) cents per page for the copies.[36]

When the association does not have a copy machine available or if the request is for more than twenty-five (25) pages, the association may have copies made by the management company or an outside vendor and may charge the member for the actual cost of the copying.[37] The records of the association must be maintained within the state and must be made available to members or their authorized representatives at reasonable times and places within ten (10) business days after receipt of a written request for access.[38]

The homeowners association may adopt reasonable rules governing the time, location, frequency, notice, and manner of records' inspection, but the rules must be in writing. The rules may not impose a requirement that the parcel owner give a reason or demonstrate a proper purpose for the inspection, nor may the rules limit the right to inspect the records to less than one (1) eight-hour business day per month. The homeowners association is not authorized to charge a fee for the inspection of records, but it may impose fees to cover the costs of providing members copies of the official records.[39] If the association denies access to its official records,[40] the member who is denied access is entitled to damages from the association for its willful failure to provide the records.[41]

In making the records available to the homeowners, the association has the option to do so electronically via the Internet or by allowing the records to be viewed in electronic format on a computer screen and printed upon request.[42] A member or the member's authorized representative

---

35 §720.303 (5), F.S.
36 *Id.*
37 §720.303 (5) (c), F.S.
38 §720.303(5) (a), F.S. The failure to provide access to records within ten (10) business days after receipt of a written request from a member by certified mail creates a rebuttable presumption that the association has willfully failed to provide access to the records.
39 §720.303 (5) (c), F.S.
40 §720.303 (5) (a), F.S.
41 §720.303 (5) (b), F.S.
42 §720.303 (5), F.S.

is also permitted to use a smartphone, tablet, portable scanner, or other electronic device to copy records and avoid reproduction charges by the association.[43]

Some records of the homeowners association are not accessible to members or parcel owners. These records include information obtained by the association in connection with the approval of a sale or other transfer of a parcel; Social Security numbers, e-mail addresses, telephone numbers, and other personal identification information; personnel records of association employees; medical records of community residents; computer passwords and proprietary software; and records protected by the attorney-client privilege prepared by the association attorney for pending or imminent litigation.[44]

6.7   Financial Obligations. Every parcel owner, regardless of how title to the property has been acquired, including purchase at a judicial sale, is liable for all assessments or amenity fees which come due while he or she is the owner.[45] Assessments for the community's operations are levied pursuant to the annual budget or special assessment, and they are allocated among the individual members of the homeowners association in the manner described by the community's governing documents.[46] The liability of the owner of a parcel for assessments is limited to the amounts properly assessed against the parcel by the homeowners association.[47]

A current account of the status of each member's financial obligation to the homeowners association must be maintained as a part of the association's official records,[48] and it is available for inspection upon request.[49] Once assessed, the association has a lien on each parcel for any unpaid assessments and for attorney's fees and costs incurred by the association incident to the collection of the assessment or the enforcement of the lien.[50] Failure to pay an assessment may also result in fines or suspension of the right to vote or the right to use the recreational amenities

---

43   *Id.*
44   §720.303 (5) (c), F.S.
45   §720.301 (11) (b) 2., F.S. and §720.312, F.S.; see also *Lunohah Investments, LLC v. Gaskel,* ___
      So.3d ___, *(Fla. 5th DCA 2013), 39 Fla. L. Weekly D41 (Fla. 5th DCA 2013) holding that liability for
      assessments does not survive issuance of a tax deed.*
46   §720.303 (6), F.S. *A member may not refuse to pay a properly levied assessment because a portion of
      the budgeted funds are used to pay an unlicensed manager. Gerecitano v. Barrwood Homeowners Ass'n,
      Inc., 882 So.2d 424 (Fla. 4th DCA 2004).*
47   §720.308, F.S.
48   §720.303 (4) (j) 2., F.S.
49   §720.303 (5), F.S.
50   §720.301 (1), F.S.

and common areas of the community when the governing documents permit.[51] (See 5.10.)

Dissatisfaction with the homeowners association or the board of directors, or the quality of maintenance being performed is not a basis for withholding payment of the assessment sums due to the association.[52] Valid assessments must be paid in a timely manner, and the dissatisfaction pursued separately as permitted by the governing documents and the law. A parcel owner's duty to pay is conditioned solely on the ownership of the lot or parcel and a properly adopted assessment under the documents and the law.[53]

6.8   Sale and Transfer of the Parcel. The covenants of a homeowners association may not unreasonably restrict the right of a parcel owner to sell or transfer the owner's property,[54] including transfers by means of a gift not involving an exchange of consideration.[55] Covenants that attempt to unduly restrict a sale of property are considered to be an "improper restraint on alienation," and they have been deemed void by Florida courts.[56] When determining the validity of a covenant that places limits on the transfer of a parcel, the type of restriction, its duration, and its price limitations are considerations when determining its reasonableness.[57] A parcel owner may not, however, use the right to sell or transfer a portion of the parcel to violate the original intent of the declaration of covenants, and efforts to do so have been rejected by the courts.[58]

Prior to the sale of an individual parcel, prospective purchasers must be provided a disclosure summary of the rights and obligations incident to ownership of a parcel in the community. Any contract for the sale of a lot or parcel must refer to or incorporate the required disclosure summary. The summary must state that membership in the homeowners association is mandatory and that recorded covenants govern the use and occupancy of property. The disclosure must reveal the obligation to pay assessments which, if unpaid, may result in a lien against the parcel and any fee or rental amounts required for use of common facilities.[59] The summary must

---

51   §720.305 (2) (b), F.S.
52   §720.301 (1), F.S. and §720.3085 (1), F.S.
53   *Ocean Trail Unit Owners Ass'n v. Mead, 650 So.2d 4, 7 (Fla. 1994).*
54   *Brower v. Hubbard, 643 So.2d 28 (Fla. 4th DCA 1994).*
55   *Webster v. Ocean Reef Community Ass'n, Inc., 994 So.2d 367 (Fla. 3d DCA 2008).*
56   *Camino Gardens Ass'n, Inc. v. McKim, 612 So.2d 636 (Fla. 4th DCA 1993); see also Davis v. Geyer, 9 So.2d 727 (Fla. 1942).*
57   *Sandpiper Development and Construction, Inc. v. Rosemary Beach Land Co., 907 So.2d 684, 685 (Fla. 1st DCA 2005).*
58   *Royal Oak Landing v. Pelletier, 620 So.2d 786 (Fla. 4th DCA 1993).*
59   *Tempel v. Southern Homes of Palm Beach, LLC, 90 So.3d 848 (Fla. 3d DCA 2012).*

also disclose whether or not the recorded covenants may be amended without the approval of the association membership.[60]

Each prospective parcel owner in a new development is entitled to receive the disclosure summary from the developer,[61] and the law provides special remedies for a purchaser who has been the victim of false and misleading information published by the developer.[62] In any contract for the resale of a residential parcel, the disclosure summary must be provided by the seller.[63] The homeowners association, at its option, may provide other information requested by a prospective purchaser or lienholder, and it may charge the prospective purchaser or lienholder a reasonable fee not to exceed $150.00 plus the costs of photocopying and attorney's fees incurred in providing the responses.[64]

Purchasers of parcels governed by a homeowners association are bound by constructive notice of the restrictive covenants that are imposed upon their property.[65] The restrictions in the recorded covenants and the disclosure summary are clothed with a strong presumption of validity arising from the fact that each parcel owner purchases the parcel knowing of and accepting the restrictions imposed.[66]

6.9 Recreational and Common Facilities Leases.
The homeowners association may enter into agreements, leases, and other membership arrangements for the benefit of the parcel owners. Such agreements may include the rights to use facilities at country clubs, golf courses, marinas, and other recreational facilities, or may include interests in parking areas, conservation areas, or submerged lands. The properties do not need to be contiguous to the community, and the membership fees and expenses of operation of the properties may be considered a common expense of the association. When the agreement, lease, or membership arrangement is not created at the time of the initial recording of the community documents, the agreement or lease must be approved by an extraordinary vote of the voting interests in the community as required by the governing documents, and if no extraordinary vote is provided in the documents, the vote must be by seventy-five (75) percent of the total voting interests of the association.[67]

---

60 §720.401, F.S.; *Princeton Homes, Inc. v. Morgan, 38 So.3d 207 (Fla. 4th DCA 2010).*
61 §720.401 (1) (a), F.S. The developer is the person or entity that creates the community served by the association or succeeds to the rights and liabilities of the person or entity creating the community.
62 §720.402, F.S.
63 §720.401 (1) (a), F.S.
64 §720.303 (5) (d), F.S.
65 *Daniel v. May, 143 So.2d 536 (Fla. 2d DCA 1962).*
66 *Eastpointe Prop. Owners' Ass'n v. Cohen, supra note 2.*
67 §720.31 (6), F.S.

The law imposes certain restrictions on and grants certain rights to the members concerning any lease for recreational or other commonly used facilities entered into by the developer-controlled association after June 15, 1995. When the lease has been entered into by the members or the homeowners association before control of the association is turned over to the members other than the developer, the lease may not contain a rent escalation clause based upon a nationally recognized commodity or consumer index. If such a clause is included in a lease entered into after June 15, 1995, the clause is unenforceable.[68] The lease must also extend certain rights to the members of the homeowners association to acquire the leased property through the association.

When the owner of the leased facilities wishes to sell the property, it may not be offered for sale unless the association is first granted a ninety (90) day option to purchase the property. Within the option period, a purchase contract must be executed by the parties or the owner of the facility may sell the property to another party.[69]

If the owner of the facilities receives an unsolicited offer to purchase the property that the owner intends to consider or make a counteroffer, the owner is obligated to notify the homeowners association that the offer has been received. The notice must be mailed to the president of the association,[70] and it must disclose the purchase price and the material terms and conditions of the proposed sale. The facility owner is not obligated to sell the property to the association, but the owner is obligated to consider any purchase offer that is made by the homeowners association.[71]

6.10 Display of Flags. Florida law makes specific provision for the display of the United States flag and the official flag of the State of Florida by property owners in the community, and the declaration of covenants, articles of incorporation, and bylaws of the homeowners association may not preclude such a display. On Memorial Day, Flag Day, Independence Day, Veterans Day, and Armed Forces Day, members may also display official flags of the United States Army, Navy, Air Force, Marine Corps, or Coast Guard.[72]

Authorized flags must be displayed in a respectful manner, and the association may establish reasonable standards governing the size,

---

68   §720.31 (5), F.S.
69   *Id.*
70   §720.31 (3), F.S.
71   §720.31 (2), F.S.
72   §720.304 (2), F.S.; see also *Gerber v. Longboat Harbour North Condominium, Inc., 724 F.Supp. 884 (M.D. Fla. 1989).*

placement, and safety of the display, consistent with Title 36 U.S.C., Chapter 10, and any applicable local ordinances.[73] Official flags of the designated branches of the United States military may not be larger than four (4) feet by six (6) feet and must be portable and removable.[74] The flagpole and display must be in compliance with applicable building codes, zoning setbacks, and locational criteria in the community's governing documents.[75]

6.11 Display of Signs. It is not uncommon to find provisions in the governing documents of the homeowners association that restrict the placement of signs on parcels in the community. These covenant provisions are enforceable when they are clear and unambiguous,[76] and when they are consistent with the contemplated purpose of the sign restrictions.[77] Notwithstanding restrictions in the documents, however, a parcel owner is permitted by law to display a sign of reasonable size that has been provided by a contractor for security services within ten (10) feet of any entrance to the home located on the parcel.[78]

6.12 Access Ramp Construction. Notwithstanding contrary provisions in the governing documents of the community, it is the right of any parcel owner to construct an access ramp for ingress and egress to the home when a resident or occupant has a disability or medical necessity requiring the modified access.[79] Prior to construction of the access ramp, the parcel owner is required to submit plans for the proposed ramp to the board of directors,[80] together with a physician's affidavit verifying the disability or medical condition.[81]

The board of directors may not reject the application, but the board may make reasonable requests to the parcel owner to modify the design in order to achieve architectural consistency with surrounding structures in community. The parcel owner is expected to provide a design for the access ramp that is as unobtrusive as possible and reasonably sized to fit the intended use.[82]

---

73   §720.3075 (3), F.S.
74   §720.304 (2) (b), F.S.
75   *Id.*
76   *Shields v. Andros Isles Property Owners Ass'n, Inc., 872 So.2d 1003 (Fla. 4th DCA 2004).*
77   *Wilson v. Rex Quality Corporation, 839 So.2d 928 (Fla. 2d DCA 2003).*
78   §720.304 (6), F.S.
79   §720.304 (5) (a), F.S.
80   *Id.*
81   §720.304 (5) (b), F.S.
82   §720.304 (5) (a), F.S.

6.13 Service Animals. In limited circumstances, state law and the Federal Fair Housing Act may override a "no pet" policy of the community when a service animal is required as a reasonable accommodation for a disabled occupant of a home.[83] In order to be entitled to the accommodation of a service animal, the occupant must have a physical or mental impairment that substantially limits the person's major life activities,[84] and the homeowners association may require the individual to provide the basis for the accommodation being requested.[85]

In making a determination on whether or not to allow a service animal, it is reasonable for the association to require the submission of an opinion from a doctor who is knowledgeable about the disability and manner in which the service animal can ameliorate the effects of the disability.[86]

6.14 SLAPP Protection and Public Participation. The law provides owners in the community with special protections to exercise their rights of free speech before institutions of government on matters related to the homeowners association and from "strategic lawsuits against public participation," known as SLAPP suits, when they engage in the participation.[87] SLAPP suits by any individual or business organization against a parcel owner are prohibited,[88] and a homeowners association is specifically prohibited from using association funds to prosecute a SLAPP suit against a parcel owner.[89]

When a SLAPP suit is filed against a parcel owner, the owner may petition the court for an order dismissing the action.[90] The court is required to set a hearing on the dismissal request at the earliest possible time, and if the parcel owner is successful, the judge may award treble damages to a prevailing owner, together with attorney's fees and costs against the person or business entity bringing the action in violation of the SLAPP suit prohibition.[91]

6.15 Electronic Transmission of Notices. With the consent of the homeowner and if permitted by the association bylaws, notices for

---

83   §413.08 (6), F.S.; §760.23, F.S.; and 42 U.S.C. §3604 (f) (3).
84   *Loren v. Sasser, 309 F.3d 1296, 1302 (11th Cir. 2002).*
85   *Hawn v. Shoreline Towers Phase I Condominium Ass'n, Inc., 347 Fed. Appx. 464 (N.D. Fla. 2009).*
86   *Prindale v. Ass'n of Apartment Owners of 2987 Kalakava, 304 F.Supp. 2d 1245, 1258–1259 (D. Hawaii 2003).*
87   §720.304 (4), F.S.
88   §720.304 (4) (a), F.S.
89   §720.304 (4) (c), F.S.
90   §720.304 (4) (b), F.S.
91   *Id.*

meetings of the board of directors, for committee meetings, and for regular and special meetings of the membership may be transmitted electronically.[92] The exception to this notice option is a meeting of the membership where the recall of a board member or members will be considered, and the electronic method of giving notice may not be used for these meetings.[93]

Electronic transmission includes both computer e-mail and facsimile transmission,[94] and notice is properly given when transmitted to the number, e-mail address, or electronic network provided to the association by the homeowner.[95] An affidavit of the secretary or other authorized agent of the association that the notice has been given by electronic transmission is, in the absence of fraud, prima facie evidence of the facts stated in the notice.[96]

---

92   §720.303 (2), F.S.
93   §720.303 (10) (c), F.S.
94   §617.01401 (6), F.S.
95   §617.0141 (3), F.S.
96   §617.0141 (8), F.S.

7

Covenants and Use
of Association Property

7.1   Covenants. Covenants governing the use of property in a community may range from the obligation to pay a portion of the common expenses to restrictions on what may be placed upon and who may occupy an individual parcel.[1] The covenants may impose limitations on the use of the property by requiring the performance of certain duties or guaranteeing certain rights to the owners of the property. Each parcel owner subject to the covenants of a homeowners association is presumed to have knowledge of the restrictions and the responsibilities that the covenants impose.[2] Additionally, each parcel owner has the right to enforce the covenants of the homeowners association against any other member, the association, or any director or officer of the association who willfully and knowingly fails to comply with the governing documents.[3]

There are essentially two categories of covenants or restrictions. The first category consists of those restrictions found in the recorded instrument subjecting the community to the jurisdiction of the homeowners association known as the "declaration of covenants."[4] The second category consists of those restrictions that are promulgated by the board of directors pursuant to authority granted by the governing documents. The first category of restrictions is clothed with a strong presumption of validity because each parcel owner purchases his or her property knowing and accepting the restrictions to be imposed.[5] Restrictions in the second category must meet a test of reasonableness which tempers the discretion of the board of directors.[6]

7.2   Covenants for Operation and Maintenance. Portions of the governing documents establish the responsibility for the operation and management of the community with the homeowners association[7] and provide for the maintenance and management of the common properties and easements in the community.[8] When the documents permit, the association may also enter and repair the property of an individual parcel owner when the owner fails to do so.[9] These covenants providing for the

---

1   *Wood v. McElvey, 296 So.2d 102 (Fla. 2d DCA 1974); Voight v. Harbour Heights Improvement Ass'n, 218 So.2d 803 (Fla. 4th DCA 1969); and Rocek v. Markowitz, 492 So.2d 460 (Fla. 5th DCA 1986).*
2   *Hagan v. Sabal Palms, Inc., 186 So.2d 302, 312–13 (Fla. 2d DCA 1966); Eastpointe Prop. Owners Ass'n v. Cohen, 505 So.2d 518 (Fla. 4th DCA 1987).*
3   §720.305 (1), F.S.; see also *Loch Haven Homeowners' Ass'n v. Nelle, 389 So.2d 697 (Fla. 2d DCA 1980).*
4   §720.301 (4), F.S.
5   *Shields v. Andros Isles Property Owners Ass'n, Inc., 872 So.2d 1003 (Fla. 4th DCA 2004).*
6   *Eastpointe Prop. Owners' Ass'n v. Cohen, supra note 2 at page 520.*
7   §720.301 (9), F.S.
8   §720.301 (1) and (4), F.S.; see also *Secret Oaks Owner's Ass'n v. D.E.P., 704 So.2d 702 (Fla. 5th DCA 1998).*
9   *Demaio v. Coco Wood Lakes Ass'n, Inc., 637 So.2d 369 (Fla. 4th DCA 1994).*

operation, maintenance, or management of the association or the property in the community must be fair and reasonable.[10]

The law governing homeowners associations imposes the same "fair and reasonable" standard on all contracts with a term in excess of ten (10) years and made by the association for operation, maintenance, or management before control of the association is turned over to the members other than the developer.[11]

The law also makes certain other restrictive covenants concerning the operation and maintenance of the community unenforceable. Association covenants may not prohibit display of the United States flag, the flag of the State of Florida, or flags of the United States Armed Services on designated holidays. The association may, however, put in place reasonable restrictions that govern the size and placement of the flag.[12] (See 6.10.) Additionally, governing documents for communities may not prohibit any parcel owner from implementing Xeriscape, or "Florida-friendly landscape,"[13] which means a quality landscape that conserves water, protects the environment, is adaptable to local conditions, and is drought tolerant.[14]

7.3   Compliance with the Covenants and Restrictions. The provisions of the declaration of covenants are enforceable as equitable servitudes, and they are covenants and restrictions with which the association, each officer and director of the association, and each parcel owner and their visitors and guests must comply.[15] The restrictions found in the declaration are afforded a strong presumption of validity, and reasonable restrictions will be enforced by the courts in accordance with their clear and ordinary meaning.[16] The declaration of covenants is also binding upon the developer and upon each subsequent parcel owner in the community.[17]

The uniqueness of community living and the resultant necessity for a greater degree of control over the rights of the individual parcel owners than might be tolerated given more traditional forms of property ownership is one of the basic principles of the homeowners association

---

10   §720.309, F.S.
11   *Id.*
12   §720.304 (2), F.S.; see also §720.3075 (3), F.S.
13   §720.3075 (4), F.S.
14   §373.185 (1) (b), F.S.
15   §720.305 (1), F.S.
16   *Shields v. Andros Isle Property Owners Ass'n, Inc., 872 So.2d 1003, 1005-1006 (Fla. 4th DCA 2004).*
17   *Blue Reef Holding Corp., Inc. v. Coyne, 645 So.2d 1053, 1055 (Fla. 4th DCA 1994).*

concept.[18] As a matter of equity, however, the courts have refused to sustain restrictions under circumstances which render their enforcement inequitable.[19]

Although the declaration of covenants is strictly construed in favor of a parcel owner's free use of his or her property,[20] when covenants have been clearly stated, and their enforcement is not unreasonable or arbitrary, the restrictions have been determined to be valid.[21] As a general rule, reasonable, unambiguous restrictions will be enforced consistent with the intent of the parties that is expressed by the clear and ordinary meaning of the terms in the restriction.[22] When the provisions of deed restrictions are discretionary, an association is not permitted to establish standards that are more restrictive than those permitted by local building codes.[23] Neither is the association permitted to stretch the meaning of the terms used in the community's covenants when the language is otherwise clear and unambiguous.[24]

All valid provisions of the declaration of covenants relating to a parcel that has been sold for taxes or special assessments survive the sale. The covenants are enforceable after the issuance of a tax deed or upon foreclosure of an assessment to the same extent that they would be enforceable by or against a voluntary purchaser of the parcel.[25]

A homeowners association may also preserve the community's covenants and restrictions under Florida's Marketable Record Title Act[26] by filing notice of the extension of the covenants with the Clerk of the Circuit Court. The notice and extension must be approved by a two-thirds vote of the board of directors at a meeting where a quorum is present and notice has been provided to each member of the association at least 7 days prior to the meeting.[27] The declaration of covenants may also be revived

---

18   *Belle Terre Ass'n Inc. v. Brosch, 216 So.2d 462 (Fla. 2d DCA 1968); see also Monahan v. Homeowner's of La Cita, Inc., 622 So.2d 551 (Fla. 5th DCA 1993) restricting the storage of a motor home on a parcel owner's property.*

19   *Flamingo Ranch Estates v. Sunshine Ranches Homeowners' Ass'n, 303 So.2d 665 (Fla. 4th DCA 1974).*

20   *Moore v. Stevens, 106 So.2d 901 (Fla. 1925); see also Moss v. Inverness Highlands Civic Ass'n, 521 So.2d 359 (Fla. 5th DCA 1988); Monahan v. Homeowner's of La Cita, Inc., supra note 18.*

21   *Engvalson v. Webster, 74 So.2d 113 (Fla. 1954); see also Lathan v. Hanover Woods Homeowners Ass'n, 547 So.2d 319 (Fla. 5th DCA 1989) where authority was not clearly stated and Klak v. Eagles' Reserve Homeowners Ass'n, Inc., 862 So.2d 947 (Fla. 2d DCA 2004) where court did not apply clear meaning of covenant.*

22   *Imperial Golf Club, Inc. v. Monaco, 752 So.2d 653 (Fla. 2d DCA 2000).*

23   *Voight v. Harbour Heights Improvement Ass'n, supra note 1.*

24   *Heck v. Parkview Place Homeowners Association, Inc., 642 So.2d 1201 (Fla. 4th DCA 1994).*

25   §720.312, F.S.; see *Gainer v. Fiddlesticks County Club, Inc., 710 So.2d 76 (Fla. 2d DCA 1998).*

26   Chapter 712, F.S.

27   §712.05, F.S.; see also *Cudjoe Gardens Property Owners Assoc., Inc. v. Payne, 770 So.2d 190 (Fla. 3d DCA 2001).*

after expiring under the procedures established by Chapter 720 of the Florida Statutes.[28] (See 7.11.)

7.4 Mediation and Enforcement of the Documents. The board of directors of the homeowners association has the statutory authority to enforce the governing documents and the rules of the association when a violation occurs.[29] Each individual member of the association also has the authority to enforce the documents and the association rules.[30]

Disputes between a parcel owner and the association regarding (1) the use of or changes to the owner's parcel or the common areas, (2) covenant disputes, (3) disputes regarding meetings of the board and committees of the board, (4) meetings of the membership not involving elections, (5) access to the official records of the association, and (6) disputes regarding amendments to the governing documents must be subject to an offer for the parties to participate in presuit mediation before the dispute is filed in court.[31] Any petition for mediation or any petition for arbitration filed with the Department of Business and Professional Regulation tolls any statute of limitations that might be applicable to the dispute,[32] and if emergency relief is required, temporary injunctive relief may be sought in court prior to the presuit mediation requirements.[33]

Election disputes and disputes over the recall of a member or members of the board of directors are not eligible for mediation, and these matters must be submitted to the Department of Business and Professional Regulation for mandatory binding arbitration.[34] Disputes involving the collection of assessments or other financial obligations or actions to enforce a prior mediation agreement are also not eligible for presuit mediation and are resolved pursuant to the separate procedures provide by statute.[35] (See 5.9.)

Mediation proceedings are initiated by the aggrieved party who is required to serve a written offer to participate in the process by certified

---

28   §720.403 through §720.407, F.S.
29   Prior to the 1995 law authorizing an association to enforce community documents, the Supreme Court of Florida declined to permit an association standing to enforce covenants when it was not the direct successor to the developer's interests or expressly assigned the right to enforce the documents. See *Palm Point Property Owners' Association of Charlotte County, Inc. v. Pisarski, 626 So.2d 195 (Fla. 1993); see also Homeowner's Ass'n of Overlook, Inc. v. Seabrooke Homeowner's Ass'n, Inc., 62 So.3d 667 (Fla. 4th DCA 2011).*
30   §720.305 (1), F.S.
31   §720.311 (2) (a), F.S.
32   §720.311 (1), F.S.
33   §720.311 (2) (a), F.S.
34   §720.306 (9), F.S. and §720.303 (10), F.S.
35   §720.311 (2) (a), F.S. In any dispute subject to presuit mediation where emergency relief is required, temporary relief sought in court without complying with the presuit mediation requirements.

mail,[36] using the format provided in the statute and identifying the specific nature of the dispute and the basis for the alleged violation.[37] If the opposing party fails to respond within twenty (20) days, refuses to mediate, or fails to participate as the statute requires, the dispute may proceed to court.[38] In mediation, the costs for the mediator are shared equally by the parties and each party assumes responsibility for their respective attorney's fees and costs.[39] All communications in the mediation proceedings are confidential and a participant may not disclose mediation communications to a person who is not a participant in the proceedings.[40]

If presuit mediation is not successful in resolving all the issues between the parties, the parties may file the unresolved dispute in either county or circuit court[41] or elect to enter into binding or non-binding arbitration to be conducted by the Department. If all the parties to the dispute do not agree to the arbitration following unsuccessful mediation, or if the dispute is not eligible for mediation or arbitration, the association or the member may seek relief in a court action, at law, or in equity,[42] and the prevailing party in such action is entitled to recovery of reasonable attorney's fees and costs of the proceeding.[43] A judgment for attorney's fees and costs may be considered a continuing lien preexisting the homestead exemption if it is provided for in the community documents.[44] At any time after the filing of a complaint in court, the judge may also order the parties to the dispute to enter into further mediation or arbitration proceedings.[45]

7.5 Enforcement Sanctions and Penalties. When a member is more than ninety (90) days delinquent in a monetary obligation due to the association, the board of directors may suspend the rights of a member or a member's tenants or guests to use the common areas or recreational facilities for violation of the documents or rules of the association until the monetary obligation is paid. The association may also impose reasonable fines, not to exceed $100 per violation, against any member, tenant, or

36   §720.311 (2) (b), F.S.
37   §720.311 (2) (a), F.S.
38   §720.311 (2) (b), F.S.
39   *Id.*
40   §44.401 through §44.406, F.S.
41   §34.01 (1) (d), F.S.
42   §720.311 (2) (b), F.S.
43   *Id.; Parton v. Palomino Lakes Property Owners Ass'n, Inc., 928 So.2d 449 (Fla. 2d DCA 2006); Zerquera v. Centennial Homeowners' Ass'n, Inc., 752 So.2d 694 (Fla. 3d DCA 2000). See also Loch Ness Homeowners Ass'n v. Pelaez, 730 So.2d 380 (Fla. 3d DCA 1999) citing Pelican Bay Homeowners Ass'n, Inc. v. Sedita, 724 So.2d 684 (Fla. 5th DCA 1999).*
44   *Andres v. Indian Creek Phase III-B Homeowner's Ass'n, 901 So.2d 182 (Fla. 4th DCA 2005).*
45   §720.311, F.S.

guest violating the rules or the governing documents. An authorized fine may be levied on the basis of each day of a continuing violation, except that the total fine cannot exceed $1,000 in the aggregate unless otherwise provided in the governing documents, and the fine cannot become a lien against the parcel.[46]

Prior to imposing either a fine or suspension, a hearing must be held to afford the alleged violator an opportunity to be heard on the issue. At least fourteen (14) days' notice of the hearing must be given, and the hearing must be held before a committee of at least three (3) members of the homeowners association appointed by the board of directors who are not officers, directors, or employees of the association or the spouse, parent, child, brother, or sister of an officer, director, or employee of the association. A majority of the committee must affirmatively vote to impose the fine or suspension,[47] and no suspension of the common-area-use rights may impair the right of an owner or tenant to have vehicular or pedestrian ingress and egress to and from the community.[48]

7.6 Notice of Violation and Uniform, Timely Enforcement. The

recorded declaration of covenants and the other documents governing the community are basically an elaborate set of contract terms.[49] Each owner is protected by the contract and may insist on the enforcement of the terms of the documents, which protect the individual owner's rights in a uniform and timely manner.[50] Under some circumstances, the homeowners association may be liable for its failure to enforce covenants governing the community or for its decision to waive covenants or restrictions.[51]

The doctrines of estoppel and laches are applicable against a person who sits by and watches while his or her rights or property are encroached upon.[52] Equitable estoppel is a basic concept of fairness that results in a forfeiture of the enforcement rights when they are not used in a timely fashion. Once knowledge of a violation is obtained, enforcement

---

46   §720.305 (2), F.S.

47   §720.305 (2) (b), F.S.; see also *Tahiti Beach Homeowners Ass'n v. Pfeffer, 52 So.3d 808 (Fla. 3d DCA 2011)*.

48   §720.305 (2) (c), F.S.

49   *Silver Blue Lakes Apartments v. Silver Blue Lake Homeowners' Ass'n, 245 So.2d 609 (Fla. 1971) ("The theory adopted in this state is that the contract which embodies the restriction may be enforced against both the promisor and those taking from him with notice, thereby including amongst those who may enforce the obligation not only the promise, but those who take from him and those in the neighborhood who may be considered as beneficiaries of the contract.").*

50   *Imperial Golf Club, Inc. v. Monaco, supra note 22.*

51   *Barefield v. Lafayette Oaks Homes Ass'n, 422 So.2d 969 (Fla. 1st DCA 1982). See also Estates of Fort Lauderdale Property Owners' Ass'n v. Kalet, 492 So.2d 1340 (Fla. 4th DCA 1986) providing for enforcement after transition from developer control.*

52   *Monell v. Golfview Road Ass'n, 359 So.2d 2 (Fla. 4th DCA 1978).*

procedures must be implemented without unreasonable delay. If this does not occur in a timely manner, the rights of a parcel owner or the homeowners association to enforce the covenants may be lost.

There is no specific definition for "timely enforcement," and the facts of each case will determine whether the response by the enforcing authority was timely and reasonable under the circumstances.[53] To avoid the issue of untimely enforcement, procedures for prompt response to violations of the community's documents should be adopted and followed by the board of directors.[54]

Uniform treatment of community residents is also essential to successful enforcement of the governing documents. The enforcement procedures of the homeowners association must be uniform, reasonable, and consistent, or they can be attacked as arbitrary and capricious, and enforcement will be unsuccessful. When a parcel owner challenges the enforcement of covenants, the owner has the burden to prove the defenses that preclude enforcement, such as a claim that the enforcing authority has acted in an unreasonable or arbitrary manner.[55] If an owner seeks to have the association enforce the covenants against another, the owner has the burden to show that enforcement by the association is not discretionary.[56]

7.7 Age and Occupancy Limitations. Restrictions limiting the use of parcels within a planned development for residential purposes are enforceable and commonplace. Covenants prohibiting the further subdivision of a residential parcel[57] and restricting a parcel to only one residence have also been sustained.[58] A covenant restricting a parcel "for residence only," however, does not prohibit short-term rentals[59] or the erection of a multi-family residential facility.[60] It has been held that a "residential purposes" restriction does not prohibit parcel owners from renting rooms as an adult congregate living facility when the owner of the parcel is also in occupancy.[61] Under a similar covenant where the owner was not in occupancy, however, use of the parcel for an adult congregate living facility was deemed to be a commercial venture, and its

---

53   Enforcement proceedings are considered legal or equitable actions on a contract, and a five-year statute
       of limitations applies pursuant to§95.11 (2) (b), F.S. *Fox v. Madsen, 12 So.3d 1261 (Fla. 4th DCA 2009).*
54   *Loch Ness Homeowners Ass'n, Inc. v. Pelaez, supra note 43.*
55   *Killearn Acres Homeowners v. Keever, 595 So.2d 1019 (Fla. 1st DCA 1992).*
56   *Heath v. Bear Island Homeowners Ass'n, Inc., 76 So.3d 39 (Fla. 4th DCA 2011).*
57   *Belle Terre Ass'n v. Brosch, 216 So.2d 463 (Fla. 2d DCA 1969).*
58   *Mayes v. Hale, 82 Fla. 35, 89 So. 364 (Fla. 1921). See also Dornbach v. Holley, 854 So.2d 211(Fla. 2d
       DCA 2002) permitting a community residential home and overriding the community covenants.*
59   *Berry v. Teves, 752 So.2d 112 (Fla. 2d DCA 2000).*
60   *Don Cesar Property Owners Corp. v. Gallagher, 452 So.2d 1047 (Fla. 2d DCA 1984).*
61   *Moss v. Inverness Highlands South and West Civic Ass'n, Inc., 521 So.2d 359 (Fla. 5th DCA 1988).*

continuation as a congregate facility was enjoined.[62]

Some residential communities are intended for senior adult occupancy only. Preserving the common scheme and continuity for a senior adult community necessitates the enforcement of age restrictions that prohibit children from becoming permanent residents in the community. Age restrictions are not constitutionally prohibited unless they are unreasonably or arbitrarily applied. Such restrictions are, however, governed by the Federal Fair Housing Act.[63] The Fair Housing Amendments Act of 1988 prohibits discrimination based upon age unless occupancy is intended for and restricted to persons 62 years of age or older, or when occupancy is restricted to residents 55 years of age or older and at least 80% of the parcels are occupied by at least one person 55 years of age or over.[64]

A community claiming senior-adult status is required to register with the Florida Commission on Human Relations, stating that the community complies with the appropriate requirements to qualify for the status. The filing must be submitted in writing on the letterhead of the community and signed by the association president. The registration must be renewed biennially from the date of the original filing. The Commission is authorized to charge a registration fee, not to exceed $20.00 for the filing, and the filings are public records and available in the Commission's Internet website. An administrative fine, not to exceed $500.00, may be imposed against a community that knowingly submits false information in its filing.[65]

As with the enforcement of all restrictions, uniformity and consistency are important. Because age restrictions clearly have the potential of excluding persons from the community, adequate notice and timely enforcement must be consistently provided. Careful compliance with the Federal Fair Housing Act is also essential if an adult community is to be successfully preserved.

Deed restrictions and covenants restricting ownership or occupancy of a parcel based upon racial or religious grounds are not enforceable.[66] Any element of judicial enforcement of such a discriminatory covenant is

---

62   *Laursen v. Giolli, 549 So.2d 1174 (Fla. 2d DCA 1989).*
63   *White Egret Condominium v. Franklin, 379 So.2d 346 (Fla. 1979); see Pomcrantz v. Woodlands Section 8 Ass'n, 479 So.2d 794 (Fla. 4th DCA 1986); and Rocek v. Markowitz, supra note 1, applying White Egret to homeowners' associations.*
64   42 U.S.C. §§360l-3619; see also §760.29 (4), F.S.
65   §760.29 (4) (e), F.S.
66   *Harris v. Sunset Island Property Owners, 116 So.2d 622 (Fla. 1959); Shelley v. Kraemer, 334 U.S. 1, 685 S.Ct. 836 (1948).*

considered "state action" and thus a violation of the Federal Civil Rights Act.[67]

7.8   Lease and Rental Restrictions. Many community governing documents contain restrictions for the lease and rental of parcels, and the association has the power and duty to enforce the restrictions.[68] Lease and rental restrictions that are clearly stated in the governing documents and uniformly enforced promote the residential character of the community and do not inherently violate any fundamental rights of the owner of the parcel.[69] When the rules or restrictions are unclear or when they are improperly applied, however, the objective may be lost. Tenants, guests, and invitees of an owner occupying a parcel or using the common areas are required to comply with the governing documents of the community and the rules and regulations of the association.[70]

7.9   Sale and Transfer Restrictions. Occasionally, community governing documents will contain restrictions on the sale or transfer of parcels in the community, and Florida courts have permitted the enforcement of such restrictions as long as they are for a lawful purpose,[71] reasonable,[72] and clearly expressed in the covenants.[73] When a covenant places an unreasonable restriction on the sale of property, however, it is considered an "improper restraint on alienation" and is not enforceable in the courts.[74]

7.10   Amendments to the Governing Documents. Because the governing documents establish the character and scheme for the community and the rights of those owning property in the community, there are restrictions on how the documents may be changed. Traditionally, the restrictions and the required vote for approving amendments to the

---

67   42 U.S.C. §1983; see also *Quail Creek Property Owners v. Hunter, 538 So.2d 1288 (Fla. 2d DCA 1988).*

68   §720.303 (1), F.S.

69   *Woodside Village Condominium v. Jahren, 754 So.2d 831, 832 (Fla. 2d DCA 2000); see also Woodside Village Condominium Assoc. v. Jahren, 806 So.2d 452 (Fla. 2002) regarding amendments to rental restrictions.*

70   §720.305 (1), F.S.

71   *Aquarian Foundation, Inc. v. Sholom House, Inc., 448 So.2d 1166, 1168 (Fla. 3d DCA 1984).*

72   *Indian River Colony Club, Inc. v. Bagg, 727 So.2d 1143 (5th DCA 1999); Chianese v. Culley, 397 Fed. Supp. 1344 (USDC Fla. SD 1975).*

73   *Aquarian Foundation, Inc. v. Sholom House, Inc., supra note 71.*

74   *Camino Gardens Ass'n, Inc. v. McKim, 612 So.2d 637 (Fla. 4th DCA 1993); Inglehart v. Phillips, 383 So.2d 610 (Fla. 1980).*

articles of incorporation,[75] bylaws,[76] and the declaration of covenants[77] are contained within the documents.

Where it is unclear from the documents whether an amendment can be adopted by the board of directors or requires approval by the membership, membership approval has been deemed necessary.[78] When the governing documents do not set forth the vote required for amendments, the law requires that an affirmative vote of two-thirds of the voting interests in the association be obtained. If the proposed amendment materially or adversely alters an owner's voting interests or increases the percentage by which a parcel shares in the common expenses, the owner and the record owners of liens on the affected parcel must join in the execution of the amendment.[79] When the required approval of the association membership specified in the documents and the law is attained, the amendment is recorded in the public records and validly enacted.[80]

Within thirty (30) days after the recording, the association is required to provide copies of the amendment to the members of the association unless a copy of the proposed amendment was provided to the members prior to the vote and the amendment was not changed before the vote. In that circumstance, the association may provide notice of the recording with the official recording information in lieu of providing an actual copy of the amendment. After receiving the notice, any member may request a copy of the amendment in writing and the association must provide the copy at no charge.[81]

If the developer has reserved the power in the declaration of covenants to amend or modify the restrictions governing the community, the power must be exercised in a reasonable manner so as not to destroy the general plan of development.[82] The developer may not use the "reserved power to amend" to prejudice the rights of parcel owners to use and enjoy the benefits of the common property without the consent of the owners.[83] Further, without the consent of all affected parcel owners,

---

75 §617.0202 (2) (b) and §617.1002, F.S.
76 §617.0206, F.S.; see also *Westwood Community Town Ass'n v. Lewis, 687 So.2d 296 (Fla. 4th DCA 1997)* holding that an amendment to bylaws cannot supersede provisions of the recorded covenants.
77 *Holiday Pines Prop. Owners v. Wetherington, 596 So.2d 84 (Fla. 4th DCA 1992); see also Palma v. Townhomes of Oriole Ass'n, Inc., 610 So.2d 112 (Fla. 4th DCA 1992) and Isle of Catalina Homeowners Ass'n, Inc v. Pardee, 739 So.2d 664 (Fla. 5th DCA 1999).*
78 *Palma v. Townhomes of Oriole Ass'n, Inc., supra note 77.*
79 §720.306 (1) (b) and (c), F.S.
80 *Holiday Pines Prop. Owners v. Wetherington, supra note 77; see also Zerquera v. Centennial Homeowners' Ass'n, Inc., 721 So.2d 751 (Fla. 3d DCA 1998).*
81 §720.306 (1) (b), F.S.
82 *Flescher v. Oak Run Associates, Ltd., 111 So.3d 929 (Fla 5th DCA 2013;Nelle v. Loch Haven Homeowners' Ass'n, 413 So.2d 28,29 (Fla. 1982).*
83 *Blue Reef Holding Corp., Inc. v. Coyne, 645 So.2d 1053 (Fla. 4th DCA 1994).*

neither the developer[84] nor the association[85] is permitted to radically change the community scheme[86] or reduce the size of the common area or limit the access of owners to it.[87]

7.11 Revival of the Governing Documents.

The governing documents in some Florida homeowners associations provide for an expiration of the community covenants after a specified number of years. Community covenants may also expire by operation of law by terms of the Marketable Record Title Act.[88] Residents in these communities have the option to extend the covenants (see 7.3) or revive the governing documents after the expiration date by following the procedural steps found in Chapter 720 of the Florida Statutes.[89]

A proposal to revive the community documents must be initiated by an organizing committee of not less than three (3) parcel owners in the community. The committee must prepare a complete set of the documents that are proposed for revival and identify the parcel owners to be subject to the revived documents. The proposed documents, together with a graphic depiction of the affected property must be presented to all of the affected owners by mail or hand delivery at least fourteen (14) days before approval of the revived documents is to be considered.[90]

A majority of the affected property owners may agree in writing to revive the governing documents, or the affected parcel owners may vote to revive the documents at a properly called membership meeting of the property owners. (See 2.4.) If the required approval is obtained at a membership meeting, the proof of notice of the meeting and the minutes of the meeting must be certified by an attorney or a court reporter.[91]

Once approved by a majority of the affected property owners, the governing documents and the documentation supporting the revival of the documents must be forwarded by the organizing committee to the Department of Economic Opportunity.[92] Once the Department determines that the proper procedures were followed, the organizing committee will be notified to record the revived community documents in the official

---

84   *Id.*
85   *Lewis v. S & T Anchorage, Inc., 616 So.2d 478 (Fla. 3d DCA 1993).*
86   *Klinow v. Island Court at Boca West Property Owners' Ass'n, Inc., 64 So.3d 177, 180 (Fla. 4th DCA 2011).*
87   *S & T Anchorage, Inc. v. Lewis, 575 So.2d 696 (Fla. 3d DCA 1991).*
88   Chapter 712, F.S.
89   §720.403 and §720.404, F.S. See also §712.11, F.S. permitting documents to be revised in a community without a mandatory homeowners' association.
90   §720.405, F.S.
91   §720.405 (6), F.S.
92   §720.406, F.S.

records of the county where the property is located. The committee must thereafter deliver a recorded copy of the documents to all of the affected parcel owners. The revived governing documents are effective upon recording.[93]

7.12 Towing of Unauthorized Vehicles. The Florida Statutes impose specific requirements on a homeowners association or its designated representative prior to the towing of an improperly parked motor vehicle if the association is to avoid liability for its acts.[94] The owner of the improperly parked vehicle must personally be notified that parking is not authorized, or the area must be prominently posted at each driveway access within five feet of the public right of way line advising motorists that the area is a "tow-away zone." The notice on the signs must have light-reflective letters on contrasting background at least two inches in height, and the words "tow-away zone" must be included on the signs in not less than four-inch letters. The sign structures must be at least four feet above ground level. If the homeowners association has a contract with a towing company, the name and telephone number of the company must also appear on the sign.[95]

When an unauthorized vehicle is actually removed from the property in the community, it must be stored at a site within ten (10) miles of the property in a county having a population of more than 500,000 people and within fifteen (15) miles of the property in a county having a population of less than 500,000 people. The person towing the motor vehicle must notify the appropriate law enforcement officials within thirty (30) minutes of the towing and provide to them a description of the vehicle, the model, and license plate number.

If the owner of the vehicle arrives at the scene prior to towing of the motor vehicle, the vehicle must be disconnected, and the owner shall be liable for the payment of a reasonable service fee. If the homeowners association causes a vehicle to be removed improperly, it is liable for the cost of removal, transportation, and storage as well as damages resulting from the removal of the vehicle including any attorney's fees and court costs.[96]

7.13 Private Roadways. In communities that have private roadways, the association must operate and maintain the rights-of-way as required in

---

93 §720.407, F.S.
94 §715.07 (2), F.S.
95 §715.07 (2) (a), F.S.
96 §715.07 (4), F.S.

the governing documents to avoid actions in law or equity resulting from their failure or refusal to carry out these responsibilities.[97] Associations also need to be sensitive to the fact that an accident or injury resulting from an improperly maintained roadway for which the association is responsible can expose the association and its membership to claims for damages for the association's negligence.[98] When permitted by the governing documents, the association may suspend the rights of a member to use the common areas for violation of the documents, but the suspension cannot impair the right of an owner or a tenant to have vehicular and pedestrian access to the owner's home, including the right to park a vehicle in permitted areas.[99]

When the roads in the community are private, the board of directors of the homeowners association, by majority vote, may elect to have state traffic laws enforced by local law enforcement agencies on the private roadways.[100] Jurisdiction over the community's private roadways is implemented by written agreement, which must make provision for the costs of traffic control and liability insurance. The agreement may also provide for the installation of multiparty stop signs and the regulation of access by means of security devices and personnel.[101]

If the roadways in a community are dedicated to the county and the homeowners desire to convert the roadways to private ownership, they may request the county to convey the roadways to the association. To make this change, the association must request the conveyance in writing and at least four-fifths of the owners must consent in writing. The county may then abandon the roads and convey them to the homeowners association for the purposes of converting the subdivision to a gated neighborhood with restricted public access to the roadways. The association must have the authority in the governing documents and must carry out the responsibility and agree to assume responsibility for the ongoing maintenance and repair of the roadways, as well as any drainage structures, street lighting and sidewalks. Upon conveyance from the county, the homeowners association holds the roadways in trust for the benefit of the owners of property in the community and must operate and maintain the roadways for the use and benefit of the owners and their guests.[102]

---

97   §720.305 (1), F.S.
98   *National Title Insurance Co. v. Lakeshore I Condominium Assoc., Inc., 691 So.2d 1104 (Fla. 3d DCA 1997); Winston Towers 100 Assoc., Inc. v. De Carlo, 481 So.2d 1261 (Fla. 3d DCA 1986).*
99   §720.305 (1) (c), F.S.
100   §316.006 (2) (b) and (3) (b), F.S.
101   *Id.*
102   §316.006 (3) (c), F.S. and §336.125, F.S.

The existence of an easement agreement granting access to the roadways by others who are not members of the association does not necessarily preclude the association from installing and maintaining gated access to the roadways.[103] The ability of the association to maintain gated access is dependent on whether or not the gate unreasonably interferes with the easement holders' rights of passage.[104]

7.14 Penny-ante Gambling. Unless prohibited by the governing documents, limited gambling is permitted in the common areas of the community or in an individual residence. Games permitted include poker, pinochle, bridge, rummy, canasta, hearts, dominoes, and mah-jongg.[105] Jackpots are limited to $10 per game, the host must be present during the game, and the host is not permitted to receive any commission. Participants may not be solicited to play and all must be over eighteen (18) years of age. No debt incurred in a game is legally enforceable.[106]

The homeowners association or an owner participating in the game shall not have any civil liability for damages if the restrictions of the law related to penny-ante gambling are properly followed.[107] Games that are conducted outside the definition and restrictions prescribed for penny-ante games, however, are considered illegal, and anyone exercising direct or indirect control over the illegal activity may be exposed to criminal liability, and the liability can extend to the homeowners association and its officers and agents when the common areas of the community are used for the games.[108]

7.15 Association Emergency Powers. In response to a declared emergency in the locale where the community is located,[109] the board of directors may exercise extraordinary emergency powers[110] to protect the safety and welfare of the association and the parcel owners[111] unless specifically prohibited by the community covenants. Pursuant to the special powers, the board of directors can implement an emergency disaster plan; require evacuation of the property; shut down the elevators, electricity, and other utility systems on the property; and declare the association unavailable for entry and occupancy.[112] The emergency

---

103   *BHB Development v. Bonefish Yacht Club Homeowners Ass'n, 691 So.2d 1174 (Fla. 3d DCA 1997).*
104   *Sandlake Residences, LLC v. Ogilvie, 951 So.2d 117, 120 (Fla. 5th DCA 2007).*
105   §849.085 (2) (a), F.S.
106   §849.085 (5), F.S.
107   *Id.*
108   §849.01, F.S.
109   The emergency must be declared by the Governor under § 252.36, F.S.
110   §720.316 (1), F.S.
111   §720.316 (2), F.S.
112   §720.316 (1) (f), (g) and (h), F.S.

powers authorize the board to mitigate further damage to the property by removing debris and water-damaged components of the building, and the powers permit the board to contract for services to prevent further damage to the condominium and make emergency repairs to the property.[113]

The Act also provides for administrative flexibility during times of a declared emergency. Meetings can be canceled and rescheduled, and meeting notices are required only as practicable and may be given by alternative means.[114] The association is permitted to relocate its principal administrative office and appoint special officers to function during the state of emergency,[115] and the board may levy special assessments, borrow funds and pledge association assets to carry out its functions during the declared emergency without a vote of the membership.[116]

The special emergency powers must be exercised in good faith, with prudent care, and in the best interests of the association.[117] The duration of the emergency powers is limited to the time reasonably necessary to protect the health and safety of the parcel owners, to mitigate further damage to the association property, and to make emergency repairs as appropriate.[118]

---

113   §720.316 (1) (e) and (i), F.S.
114   §720.316 (1) (a) and (b), F.S.
115   §720.316 (1) (c) and (d), F.S.
116   §720.316 (1) (j) and (k), F.S.
117   §617.0830, F.S.
118   §720.316 (2), F.S.

8
Architectural Control and Standards

8.1 Architectural Standards. The authority of a homeowners association to review and approve the architectural plans and specifications for improvements on a parcel in the community is permitted to the extent that the authority is specifically stated or reasonably inferred in the declaration of covenants or published guidelines authorized by the declaration.[1] A purchaser's notice of these building restrictions may be derived from the deed restrictions themselves or by the visible presence of a unified scheme of development.[2] Florida law has consistently upheld the power of homeowners associations to enforce building restrictions,[3] even when sales agents misrepresent the extent of or enforcement of the restrictions.[4]

If declaration of covenants provides options for the building materials, the size and design of the structure, or the location of the building or improvements on the parcel, the owner is entitled to select from the options provided in the declaration, and the association may not restrict the choices by the parcel owner.[5] Unless the declaration of covenants provides otherwise, when a parcel is bounded by a roadway on two sides, the parcel shall have only one (1) front building setback limitation.[6]

8.2 Unauthorized Structures. If a parcel owner has erected or placed a structure on his or her property in violation of clearly expressed restrictions in the covenants, the homeowners association or another owner is fully empowered to seek the removal of the structure in court that is in violation of the restrictions.[7] The association may also maintain an enforcement action to preserve the exterior appearance of buildings and structures that are otherwise permitted under the covenants.[8] A policy restricting buildings or structures that is inconsistent with the rights of a parcel owner expressed in the declaration of covenants, however, may not be enforced by the association, whether uniformly applied or not.[9]

---

1   §720.3035 (1), F.S.
2   *Young v. Tortoise Island Homeowners' Ass'n, 511 So.2d 381 (Fla. 5th DCA 1987).*
3   *Id. See also Coral Gables Investment v. Graham Companies, 528 So.2d 989 (Fla. 3d DCA 1988); Engvalson et ux v. Webster, 74 So.2d 113 (Fla. 1954).*
4   *Esplanade Patio Homes Homeowners' Assoc. v. Rolle, 613 So.2d 531 (Fla. 3d DCA 1993).*
5   §720.3035 (2), F.S.
6   §720.3035 (3), F.S.
7   "Where contracts are clear and unambiguous, they should be construed as written, and the court can give it no other meaning." *Heck v. Parkview Place Homeowners Association, Inc., 642 So.2d 1201 (Fla. 4th DCA 1994).*
8   See *Lake Charleston Maintenance Ass'n, Inc. v. Farrell, 16 So.3d 182 (Fla. 4th DCA 2009).*
9   §720.3035 (5), F.S.; see also *Wenger v. Breakwater Homeowners Ass'n Inc., 423 So.2d 619 (Fla. 4th DCA 1982).*

Courts have ordered the removal of structures and improvements not authorized by the community's declaration of covenants, including unauthorized carports,[10] porches,[11] decks,[12] satellite dishes,[13] ham radio antennas,[14] radio tower/antennas,[15] docks,[16] exterior awnings,[17] sheds and similar structures,[18] improper fencing,[19] concrete walls,[20] an exterior wall plaque,[21] and a portion of a dwelling encroaching on a setback line between parcels.[22] The role of the association in enforcing the restrictions also applies to holding the developer accountable for any construction defects in the common areas.[23] (See 1.4.)

8.3 Permitted Structures and Improvements.

Any restrictive covenant appearing in a community's governing documents that attempts to prohibit the installation of solar collectors, clotheslines, or other energy savings devices that are based on renewable energy resources is contrary to public policy.[24] A homeowners association may not enforce such restrictions, and in any litigation to protect the right to install energy saving devices, the prevailing party is entitled to recover court costs and reasonable attorney's fees.[25] A parcel owner may also install access ramps if a resident of the property has a medical necessity or disability that requires a ramp for ingress and egress.[26] (See 6.12.)

A community's covenants notwithstanding, the Telecommunications Act of 1996 assures each residential parcel owner access to certain television service provided by "direct broadcast satellite." In response to this mandate from Congress, the Federal Communications Commission

---

10   *Pelican Island Property Owners' Ass'n v. Murphy, 554 So.2d 1179 (Fla. 2d DCA 1989).*

11   *Europco Mgt. Co. of America v. Smith, 572 So.2d 963 (Fla. 1st DCA 1990).*

12   *Miami Lakes Civic Ass'n, Inc. v. Encinosa, 699 So.2d 271 (Fla. 3d DCA 1997).*

13   *Killearn Acres Homeowners Association, Inc. v. Keever, 595 So.2d 1019 (Fla. 1st DCA 1992); see also Esplanade Patio Homes v. Rolle, supra note 4 and Latera v. The Isle at Mission Bay Homeowners Ass'n, 655 So.2d 144, (Fla. 4th DCA 1995).*

14   *Emerald Estates Community Assoc., Inc. v. Gorodetzer, 819 So.2d 190 (Fla. 4th DCA 2002).*

15   *Brower v. Hubbard, 643 So.2d 28 (Fla. 4th DCA 1994).*

16   *Johnson v. Tlush, 468 So.2d 1023 (Fla. 4th DCA 1985); O'Brien v. Gale J. Apple, Inc., 253 So.2d 717 (Fla. 2d DCA 1971).*

17   *Eastpointe Property Owners' Ass'n Inc. v. Cohen, 504 So.2d 518 (Fla. 4th DCA 1987).*

18   *McMillan v. The Oaks of Spring Hill Homeowners' Ass'n, 754 So.2d 160 (Fla. 5th DCA 2000).*

19   *Foonberg v. Thornhill Homeowners Ass'n, Inc., 975 So.2d 601 (Fla. 4th DCA 2008); James v. Smith, 537 So.2d 1074 (Fla. 5th DCA 1989).*

20   *Velickovich v. Ricci, 391 So.2d 258 (Fla. 4th DCA 1980).*

21   *Lakeridge Greens Homeowners Assoc., Inc. v. Silberman, 765 So.2d 95 (Fla. 4th DCA 2000).*

22   *Daniel v. May, 143 So.2d 536 (Fla. 3d DCA 1962).*

23   *Strathmore Gate-East at Lake St. George Homeowners' v. Levitt Homes, 537 So.2d 657 (Fla. 2d DCA 1989). See also §§558.001-005, F.S.*

24   §163.04 (2), F.S.; *Sorrentino v. River Run Condominium Ass'n, Inc., 925 So.2d 1060 (Fla. 5th DCA 2006).*

25   §163.04 (3), F.S.

26   §720.304 (5) (a), F.S.

has adopted rules that prohibit the enforcement of covenants that restrict, delay, or unreasonably increase the cost of installation of a direct broadcast satellite dish which is less than one (1) meter in diameter. The FCC rule makes such covenants affecting property within the exclusive use and ownership of a parcel owner unenforceable.[27]

8.4   Communication Services. In addition to direct broadcast satellite service, no resident in the community may be denied access to available cable or video communication services provided by a franchised or certified service provider.[28] Other than routine installation charges and fees normally paid for the services received, a resident may not be required to pay anything of additional value when accessing these services.[29]

Communication service for residents may also be provided by a bulk service contract entered into by the homeowners association.[30] The bulk service contract may include cable television, Internet for online computer access and e-mail, telephone, and other data and information services.[31] Authority to enter into the contract may be provided for in the governing documents, or it may be exercised by the board of directors as authorized by law.[32] When the contract is entered into by the board, however, it is subject to cancellation by the members upon a majority vote at the next regular or special meeting of the membership.[33]

8.5   Uniform Community Scheme. Restrictions designed to create and maintain a uniform scheme of community development through the discretionary review of the homeowners association are presumed valid provided such review is properly conducted.[34] The review of proposed structures and improvements for conformity with uniform standards and construction criteria is deemed to be proper when it is exercised in a reasonable manner,[35] however, the restrictions must be stated or reasonably inferred from the declaration of covenants or be contained in published

---

27   §25.104, *Rules of the Federal Communications Commission implementing §207 of the Federal Telecommunications Act of 1996.*

28   §720.309 (2) (c), F.S.

29   *Id.*

30   §720.309 (2), F.S.

31   §202.11 (2), F.S.

32   §720.309 (2), F.S.

33   §720.309 (2) (a), F.S.

34   *Cohen v. Boca Woods Country Club Property Owners Ass'n, Inc., 632 So.2d 1142 (Fla. 4th DCA 1994); Young v. Tortoise Island Homeowners' Ass'n, supra note 2; Coral Gables Investment v. Graham Companies, 528 So.2d 989 (Fla. 3d DCA 1988); Voight v. Harbour Heights Improvement Ass'n, 218 So.2d 803 (Fla. 4th DCA 1969); Engvalson et ux. v Webster, supra note 3.*

35   *Id. See also Emerald Estates Community Assoc., Inc. v. Gorodetzer, supra note 14*

guidelines authorized by the declaration.[36]

Restrictions based purely on aesthetic concepts,[37] not supported by the covenants[38] and competent and substantial evidence, or establishing arbitrary standards,[39] are not valid. Whether uniformly applied or not, the homeowners association may not enforce any architectural policy or restriction that is inconsistent with the rights and privileges of a parcel owner that are set forth in the declaration of the covenants or other published guidelines authorized by the covenants.[40]

8.6   Architectural Review Committee. It is permissible for the uniform architectural scheme in the community to be enforced by the board of directors of the homeowners association or by a properly established architectural review, construction improvement, or similar committee of the association.[41] The architectural review committee may evaluate and approve plans and specifications for buildings on a parcel, and the committee may enforce standards governing the external appearance of structures and improvements on the parcels in the community to the extent permitted by the declaration of covenants.[42]

Any committee or similar body vested with the final authority to approve or disapprove architectural decisions with respect to a specific parcel of residential property owned by a member of the community must comply with all the notice and meeting procedures required of the board of directors of the homeowners association.[43] Although the meetings of the committee must be open to the members of the association, due process does not require that the affected parcel owner be afforded an opportunity to make a presentation before the decision-making body.[44] The committee may not unreasonably infringe upon the rights and privileges extended to a parcel owner in the declaration of covenants or by the published standards and guidelines.[45]

8.7   Architectural Standards and Parcel Owner Rights. Each parcel owner is entitled to the rights and privileges that are extended by

---

36   §720.3035 (1), F.S.
37   *Young v. Tortoise Island Homeowners' Ass'n, supra note 2; Coral Gables Investment v. Graham Companies, supra note 3; Voight v. Harbour Heights Improvement Ass'n, supra note 34.*
38   §720.3035 (1), F.S.
39   *Voight v. Harbour Heights Improvement Ass'n, supra note 34; Kies v. Hollub, 450 So.2d 251 (Fla. 3d DCA 1984).*
40   §720.3035 (5), F.S.
41   *Holiday Pines Prop. Owners v. Wetherington, 596 So.2d 84 (Fla. 4th DCA 1992).*
42   §720.3035 (1), F.S.
43   §720.303 (2) (a), F.S.
44   *Europco Mgt. Co. of America v. Smith, supra note 11.*
45   §720.3035 (5), F.S.; *Cohen v. Boca Woods Country Club Property Owners Ass'n, Inc., supra note 34.*

the declaration of covenants and the published guidelines and standards authorized by the declaration for the architectural use of the property.[46] A parcel owner may use the available options for material, size, design, and location for structures and improvements on the property,[47] and building setback restrictions may not be arbitrarily imposed upon the parcel of an owner.[48]

If the board of directors or an architectural review committee of the association unreasonably, knowingly, and willfully impairs the rights of a parcel owner in the application of architectural standards, the adversely affected owner is entitled to recover damages caused by the impairment. The affected owner is also entitled to recover any costs and reasonable attorney's fees incurred in preserving or restoring the rights and privileges extended to the owner by the declaration of covenants or published guidelines and standards.[49]

8.8 Architectural Standards and Local Codes. If the local county and municipal building code requires the architectural review committee of the association to approve building design plans as a prerequisite to receiving a building permit, the committee is required to comply with Florida's Government in the Sunshine Law and Public Records Law.[50] As such, meetings of the committee must be noticed and open to the public at large and not merely to members of the association.[51] Records made or received in conjunction with the committee's deliberations are open and available for inspection by the public.[52]

---

46   §720.3035 (4), F.S.
47   §720.3035 (2), F.S.
48   §720.3035 (3), F.S.
49   §720.3035 (4), F.S.
50   *Advisory Opinion of the Florida Attorney General, AGO 99-53.*
51   §286.011, F.S.
52   §119.011 (1), F.S.

9
Rights and Responsibilities of the Developer

9.1 General. The developer is traditionally the entity that creates the community by recording the governing documents and that initially offers the lots or parcels for sale in the ordinary course of business.[1] The developer may also be the person or entity that succeeds to the rights and liabilities of the person or entity that created the community by written assignment.[2] The developer assembles the initial provisions of the declaration of covenants, creates the homeowners association, and appoints the first board of directors of the association. Until the community matures and control of the board passes to the homeowners, the developer-controlled board maintains and operates the community.[3] (See 9.6.)

The developer has wide latitude in designing the content of the declaration of covenants and creating the character and concept for the community. There are certain provisions, however, that are not permitted to be included in the governing documents under the current provisions of Florida law. The provisions of the governing documents may not restrict the right of the association to sue the developer, and the developer may not reserve the right to unilaterally amend the governing documents after the homeowners assume control of the association or retain weighted voting rights in the association after transition of control occurs.[4]

9.2 Rights and Privileges of the Developer. The developer has all of the rights appurtenant to the ownership of lot or parcel in the developer's name, and the developer has the right to control the board of directors after a majority of the parcels has been sold.[5] (See 9.6.) When the governing documents permit, the developer may be excused from the assessment obligations due to the homeowners association as permitted by the statute, provided that the budget deficits are funded by the developer.[6] (See 9.4.) The developer may also reserve the right to amend or modify the declaration of covenants, but the power must be exercised in a reasonable manner and may not be used to destroy the general plan of the community or prejudice the rights of homeowners.[7] (See 7.10.)

It is the initial option of the developer to establish reserve accounts for the homeowners association, but the developer is not required to do

---

1   §720.301 (6) (a), F.S.
2   §720.301 (6) (b), F.S.
3   §720.303 (1), F.S.
4   §720.3075, F.S.
5   §720.307 (1), F.S.
6   §720.308 (1) and (2), F.S.
7   §720.3075 (5), F.S.See also *Holiday Pines Prop. Owners v. Wetherington, 596 So.2d 84 (Fla. 4th DCA 1992); and Zerquera v. Centennial Homeowners' Ass'n, Inc., 721 So.2d 751 (Fla. 3d DCA 1998).*

so.[8] If the developer does elect to create reserves for the association, the reserve funds cannot be used for other than their intended purpose by the developer-controlled board of directors unless the alternative use is also approved by a majority of all the nondeveloper voting interests at a duly called meeting at which a quorum is present.[9]

9.3 Limitations and Obligations of the Developer. When a lot or parcel is offered for sale in the community, the developer is obligated to provide a disclosure summary statement describing the governing documents and the nature of the mandatory membership in the homeowners association.[10] (See Form 10.5-0.) Advertising and promotional materials used by the developer must not be false or misleading, and any purchaser relying on false or misleading representations has a cause of action for cancellation of the purchase contract or collection from the developer of damages that result from reliance on the misinformation.[11]

During the period that the developer controls the board of directors of the homeowners association, all funds of the association must be separately maintained in the association's name, and the operating funds of the association may not be commingled with the reserve funds of the association.[12] The association funds may be used for association purposes, but may not be used by the developer to defend civil or criminal actions, administrative proceedings, or arbitration proceedings that have been filed against the developer or the directors appointed by the developer.[13] The right of indemnification from association funds for association directors does not extend to members of the board appointed by the developer, and responsibility for actions by developer-appointed directors rests with the developer.[14] (See 3.7.)

9.4 Assessment Responsibilities of the Developer. From the time of the creation of the community until the sale of parcels to a purchaser, the developer is the owner of the parcels. As the parcel owner, the developer is liable for all assessments that come due unless the developer is excused from the payment of operating expenses and

---

8   §720.303 (6) (d), F.S.
9   §720.303 (6) (h), F.S.
10   §720.401 (1) (a), F.S.
11   §720.402 (1), F.S.
12   §720.303 (8) (b), F.S.
13   §720.303 (8) (c), F.S.
14   *Id.*

assessments by the declaration of covenants.[15] If an exemption from the assessment responsibility is not provided for the lots owned by the developer in the declaration of covenants, a separate agreement between the developer and the association may establish a guarantee period, provided that it has been approved by a majority of the parcel owners other than the developer.[16]

In order to be excused from the payment of assessments, the developer is obligated to pay any operating expenses incurred during the guarantee period that exceed the assessments receivable from the other homeowners and any other income of the association.[17] Prior to turnover, the developer may not vote to waive reserves,[18] and no portions of the assessments that are designated for reserves during the guarantee period shall be used to pay operating expenses, nor shall they be used to reduce the contributions of the developer to the operating deficit.[19] The developer's guarantee extends only for the period of time that the developer remains obligated to pay the excess operating expenses of the homeowners association.[20]

During the period of developer control, the board of directors of the association may not levy a special assessment against parcel owners in the community unless the owners other than the developer approve the assessment. Approval of the special assessment must take place at a properly noticed special meeting of the membership at which a quorum is present, and the special assessment must be approved by a majority vote of the owners participating at the meeting.[21]

9.5   Recreational Amenities. When the recreational amenities serving the community are owned by the developer or by a person or entity other than the homeowners association and the parcel owners are required to pay maintenance or amenity fees directly to the developer or to another owner of recreational facilities, the developer or other owner of the facilities is required to provide a complete financial report to the homeowners. The report must include an accounting for the actual, total receipts of the fees received from the owners, and it must be provided within sixty (60) days following the end of each fiscal year. The report may be sent by mail to each parcel owner, published in a publication regularly distributed within the community, or posted in prominent

---

15   §720.308 (1), F.S.
16   §720.308 (2) (a), F.S.
17   §720.308 (4) and (5), F.S.
18   §720.303 (6) (f), F.S.
19   §720.308 (4), F.S.
20   §720.308 (1) and (2) (b), F.S.
21   §720.315, F.S.

locations within the community.[22]

    The law also imposes certain restrictions on and grants certain rights to the members concerning any lease for recreational or other commonly used facilities entered into by the developer-controlled association.[23] The lease may not contain a rent escalation clause based upon a nationally recognized commodity or consumer index,[24] and the lease must extend certain rights to the members of the homeowners association to acquire the leased property through the association.[25] (See 6.9.)

9.6 The Developer and Transition of Control.

The provisions of the statute specifically governing homeowners associations do not mandate any schedule for transition of control of the board of directors from the developer to the members for homeowners associations created prior to June 15, 1995.[26] For such associations, the developer appoints the first complete board of directors of the association, and the developer then continues to control the board under the terms prescribed by the articles of incorporation, bylaws, and other governing documents.[27]

    For homeowners associations created after June 15, 1995, the law provides a schedule of transition from developer control to control by members other than the developer. Under the statutory schedule, the members are entitled to elect at least a majority of the members of the board of directors of the association three (3) months after ninety (90) percent of the parcels in all phases of the community to be operated by the homeowners association have been conveyed to members of the association.[28] A different percentage may apply if it is required in order to comply with the requirements of any governmentally chartered entity with regard to the mortgage financing of parcels in the community, provided that this alternative transition requirement is set out in the governing documents of the community.[29]

    Within ninety (90) days of the time that the owners are entitled to elect at least a majority of the board of directors of the association, the developer must, at the developer's expense, deliver the books

---

22   §720.3086, F.S.

23   §720.31, F.S.

24   §720.31 (5), F.S.

25   §720.31 (1) and (2), F.S.

26   §720.307 (3), F.S. The exemption also extends to a homeowners association, no matter when created, if it is in a community that is included in an effective development-of-regional-impact development order that is in effect on or before June 15, 1995.

27   §720.302 (2) and §617.0803 (3), F.S.

28   §720.307 (1), F.S. "Members other than the developer" do not include builders, contractors, or others who purchase a parcel for purposes of constructing improvements on the property for resale.

29   §720.307 (1) (b), F.S.

and records of the association to the new board. The required records include the original community documents, the corporate minute book, insurance policies and other contracts of the association, resignations of the developer-directors, a roster of the current homeowners and their addresses, any governmental permits issued to the association, a list of the names and addresses (with telephone numbers) of all contractors and employees of the association, any warranties in effect at the time of transition, and any other association property.[30]

The developer must turn over the control of all funds of the association to the new board of directors and deliver to the board all of the financial records of the association, including financial statements and source documents for the statements from the date of incorporation through the date of the turnover. For homeowners associations created after December 31, 2007, the developer must also provide an audit of the association's financial records. The audit must be for the period between the date of incorporation and the date of turnover to the homeowners.[31]

During the time the board of directors is controlled by the developer, the operational procedures, record keeping, and the election and voting requirements specified by statute are applicable to the homeowners association.[32] The provisions in the law governing association operations do not, however, impair the rights of the developer to complete the community as contemplated.[33]

9.7 Organization of Owner-Controlled Board. The newly elected members of the board of directors must be prepared to select their own officers and assume their duties and control of the homeowners association immediately. (See 4.2.) The new board members will receive the association property, records, and funds for the operation of the association,[34] and one of the primary duties of the new board will be to determine both the completeness and accuracy of the records and property received from the developer. As part of their organizational duties and responsibilities, the board should also be prepared to identify potential legal causes of action that the association may have against other parties, including warranty claims for defective construction that may be present

---

30   §720.307 (3), F.S.
31   §720.307 (2) (t), F.S. The audit may be from the date of the last audit period if an audit has been done for
     each fiscal year that the association has been in existence.
32   §720.303 and §720.306, F.S.
33   §720.302 (2), F.S.
34   §720.307 (3), F.S.

in the community's common property.[35]

Finally, the new board of directors must be prepared to assume its role in the enforcement of the governing documents. Prior conduct of the developer cannot be used against the association in an attempt to show selective or arbitrary enforcement policies of the use restrictions in the documents. However, the board controlled by the owners must be prepared to establish the uniform enforcement procedures of the association once the transfer occurs if the enforceability of the governing documents is to be preserved.[36]

9.8 Common Law Warranties. The developer of the community may owe to the eventual lot or parcel owners certain duties to complete the improvements on the lots in accordance with standards reasonably expected for facilities of comparable kind and quality.[37] These implied warranties of fitness and merchantability extend to each purchaser of property from the developer, and the right to bring an action for a breach of implied warranty belongs to these owners.[38] The right of the property owners to bring such an action may be exercised in aggregate through the homeowners association when the basis of the action consists of matters that are of common interest.[39]

The criteria to determine whether the implied warranty of fitness and merchantability has been breached is an objective one, and the party asserting the breach of warranty has the burden of establishing that a reasonable person would find that the improvements were unfit for that person's ordinary or general purpose. A "personal satisfaction" test, however, is not sufficient in determining that the warranty obligation has been breached.[40] There is also no implied warranty obligation from the developer for "offsite improvements" such as streets, drainage, and other improvements not located on or under a lot or parcel.[41]

9.9 Construction Defects—Presuit Procedures. Construction defect claims against a developer, contractor, or design professional for damages to a single-family home, a multi-family residential building,

---

35   §720.303 (1), F.S.
36   *Ladner v. Plaza Del Prado Condominium Ass'n, Inc., 423 So.2d 927 (Fla. 3d DCA 1982) and Constellation Condominium Ass'n, Inc. v. Harrington, 487 So.2d 378 (Fla. 2d DCA 1985).*
37   *David v. B & J Holding Corp., 349 So.2d 676 (Fla. 3d DCA 1977) and Vantage View, Inc. v. Bali East Development Corp., 421 So.2d 728 (Fla. 4th DCA 1982)*
38   *Gable v. Silver, 264 So.2d 418 (Fla. 1972).*
39   Rule 1.221, Florida Rules of Civil Procedure.
40   *Putnam v. Roudebush, 352 So.2d 908 (Fla. 2nd DCA 1977).*
41   §553.835, F.S.

or the common areas and improvements serving the community must be submitted to presuit procedures before a claim can be filed in court. The procedures provide the opportunity to resolve the dispute to the satisfaction of the affected owners or the association by correcting the defects or by the payment of a cash settlement.

Notice of a defect claim must be served on the developer, contractor, or design professional at least 60 (sixty) days before a court action is filed. The notice must describe the claim in detail, and the contractor or design professional must be given an opportunity to inspect the defect and provide a written response to the claim within thirty (30) days. The response must be in writing, and it may (1) offer to fix the defect at no cost to the homeowners; (2) offer to settle the claim by a monetary payment together with a timetable for making the payment; or (3) dispute the claim and refuse to correct the alleged defect.[42]

If the developer, contractor, or design professional does not respond on time or settle the claim, the homeowner or the association making the claim may proceed with a court action. The homeowner or the association making the claim may also reject the settlement offer in writing and proceed in court without further notice.[43]

Before commencing any court action against any party in the name of the homeowners association—including an action based upon construction defects—involving amounts in controversy in excess of $100,000, the association must obtain the affirmative approval of a majority of the homeowners at a meeting of the membership at which a quorum is present.[44] The restriction is intended to protect the association from a commitment of extensive resources to litigation without the approval of the owners, but it is not a condition precedent to the actual filing of a lawsuit.[45]

---

42 The time periods for claims in multifamily structures containing more than twenty (20) dwelling units are longer. *See §558.004 (4), F.S.*

43 §558.01 through 558.005, F.S.

44 §720.303(1), F.S.

45 *Lake Forest Master Community Ass'n, Inc. v. Orlando Lake Forest, 10 So.3d 1187 (Fla. 5th DCA 2009).*

10

Style and Format for Association Forms and Documents

Various types of formalities accompany the operation of the homeowners association. They ensure that proper procedures are followed to protect members' rights and that members are advised of the business and finances being conducted on their behalf. Implementing these formal prerequisites for association meetings, membership voting, and actions by the directors is not complicated, but it is essential to the proper and successful operation of the association.

The forms and sample documents that follow in this chapter are designed to assist and guide those who are responsible for conducting the affairs of the homeowners association. They present the basic format for the formal documents that are used periodically by the association, and they can be adapted for use in most communities. When the bylaws of the association specify a different format or a variation in document content, the forms in this manual should yield to the requirements of the community's bylaws. Many of the forms and sample documents concern application of law or interpretation of legal principles, and the association should be prepared to seek that advice and assistance of legal counsel when faced with such issues.

INDEX OF FORMS AND DOCUMENTS

10.1 MEMBERSHIP MEETING FORMS AND SAMPLE DOCUMENTS

10.2 BOARD OF DIRECTORS' MEETINGS AND SAMPLE DOCUMENTS

10.3 OFFICER AND COMMITTEE FORMS AND SAMPLE DOCUMENTS

10.4 BUDGET AND FINANCIAL FORMS AND SAMPLE DOCUMENTS

10.5 DISCLOSURE SUMMARY FOR PROSPECTIVE PURCHASERS

CYPRESS HOMEOWNERS ASSOCIATION, INC.
A Corporation Not-for-Profit

NOTICE OF MEMBERS MEETING

NOTICE IS HEREBY GIVEN, in accordance with the Bylaws of the Cypress Homeowners Association, Inc., that the annual (special*) meeting of members will be held at the following date, time and place:

Date: January 15, 2015
Time: 7:00 p.m.
Place: Recreation Hall
Cypress Homeowners Association, Inc.
100 Cypress Lane
Cypress Springs, Florida 33444

Agenda:

1. Calling of roll and certifying of proxies.

2. Proof of notice of meeting or waiver of notice.

3. Reading and disposal of any unapproved minutes.

4. Election of inspectors of election.

5. Election of board members.

6. Reports of officers.

7. Reports of committees.
    a. Recreation Committee.
    b. Grounds Committee.

8. Unfinished business.

9. New business.

Form 10.1-0 Notice of Members Meeting

a. Consideration of amendment to association bylaws.

b. General discussion by members.

10. Adjournment.

CYPRESS HOMEOWNERS
ASSOCIATION, INC.

By:_____
Secretary

Dated: This 20th day of December, 2014.

*(The notice for a special members' meeting must state the purpose for which the meeting is called.)

CYPRESS HOMEOWNERS ASSOCIATION, INC.
A Corporation Not-for-Profit

PROOF OF NOTICE AFFIDAVIT

STATE OF FLORIDA
COUNTY OF PINELLAS

The undersigned Secretary of the Cypress Homeowners Association, Inc., being first duly sworn, deposes and says that notice of the annual (special) membership meeting was mailed or hand-delivered to each member at the address last furnished to the Association at least fourteen (14) days prior to the annual (special) meeting.

Dated this 20th day of December, 2014.

_____
Secretary

The foregoing Affidavit was acknowledged before me this 20th day of December, 2014, by Nancy Thomas, the Secretary of Cypress Homeowners Association, Inc.

_____
Notary Public

My commission expires:

CYPRESS HOMEOWNERS ASSOCIATION, INC.
A Corporation Not-for-Profit

AGENDA
MEMBERSHIP MEETING
January 15, 2015

1. Calling of roll and certifying of proxies.

2. Proof of notice of meeting or waiver of notice.

3. Reading and disposal of any unapproved minutes.

4. Election of inspectors of election.

5. Election of board members.

6. Reports of officers.

7. Reports of committees.
   a. Recreation Committee.
   b. Grounds Committee.

8. Unfinished business.

9. New business.
   a. Consideration of amendments to association bylaws.
   b. General discussion by members.

10. Adjournment.

Form 10.1-2 Agenda for Members Meeting

CYPRESS HOMEOWNERS ASSOCIATION, INC.
A Corporation Not-for-Profit

PROXY
January 15, 2015
Membership Meeting

TO: Secretary
       Cypress Homeowners Association, Inc.
       100 Cypress Lane
       Cypress Springs, Florida 33444

KNOW ALL PERSONS BY THESE PRESENTS, that the undersigned hereby appoints the Secretary of the Association or _____, attorney and agent with the power of substitution for and in the name, place, and stead of the undersigned, to vote as proxy at the membership meeting of the Association, to be held at the Recreation Hall, January 15, 2015, at 7:00 p.m., and any adjournment thereof, according to the number of votes that the undersigned would be entitled to vote if then present upon the matters set forth in the Notice of Meeting dated December 20, 2014, a copy of which has been received by the undersigned.

(In no event shall this proxy be valid for a period longer than ninety (90) days after the date of the first meeting for which it was given.)

DATED this _____ day of January, 2015.

Parcel Owner

_____

_____

Parcel Number:_____
(or Property Address)

SUBSTITUTION OF PROXY

The undersigned, appointed as proxy above, does hereby designate
_____ to substitute for me in the proxy set forth above.

Dated:_____   _____
                                Proxy

CYPRESS HOMEOWNERS ASSOCIATION, INC.
A Corporation Not-for-Profit

PROXY
January 15, 2015
Membership Meeting

KNOW ALL PERSONS BY THESE PRESENTS, that the undersigned hereby appoints the Secretary of the Association, his or her designee, or _____, attorney and agent with the power of substitution for and in the name, place, and stead of the undersigned, to vote as proxy at the membership meeting of the Association, to be held at the Recreation Hall, January 15, 2015, at 7:00 p.m., and adjournment thereof, according to the number of votes that the undersigned would be entitled to vote if then present in accordance with the specifications hereinafter made, as follows:

General Powers

I hereby authorize and instruct my proxy to use his best judgment on all matters which properly come before the meeting.

Limited Powers

I hereby specifically authorize and instruct my proxy to cast my vote in reference to the following matters only as indicated below.

1. Should the size of the board of directors be increased from seven (7) to nine (9) members?

Yes_____   No_____

2. Should the bylaws of the Association be amended to provide that the terms of directors be for two (2) years?

Yes_____   No_____

Form 10.1-4 Limited Proxy

The undersigned ratify and confirm any and all acts and things that the proxy may do or cause to be done in the premises, whether at the meeting referred to above or at any change, adjournment, or continuation of it, and revoke all prior proxies previously executed.

Dated:_____   <u>Parcel Owner</u>

Parcel Number:_____   _____

_____   _____

(or Property Address)

SUBSTITUTION OF PROXY

The undersigned, appointed as proxy above, does hereby designate __ _____ to substitute for me in the proxy set forth above.

Dated:_____   _____

                                  Proxy

(In no event shall this proxy be valid for a period longer than ninety (90) days after the date of the first meeting for which it was given.)

CYPRESS HOMEOWNERS ASSOCIATION, INC.
A Corporation Not-for-Profit

VOTING CERTIFICATE

TO: Secretary, Cypress Homeowners Association, Inc.
100 Cypress Lane
Cypress Springs, Florida 33444

KNOW ALL MEN BY THESE PRESENTS, that the undersigned are the record owners of that certain parcel in CYPRESS HOMEOWNERS ASSOCIATION, INC., shown below, and hereby constitute, appoint, and designate _____ as the voting representative for the parcel owned by said undersigned pursuant to the Bylaws of the Association.

The forenamed voting representative is hereby authorized and empowered to act in the capacity herein set forth until such time as the undersigned otherwise modifies or revokes the authority set forth in this voting certificate.

DATED this 1ˢᵗ day of December, 2014.

Parcel Owner

_____

_____

Parcel Number:

_____

(or Property Address)

CYPRESS HOMEOWNERS ASSOCIATION, INC.
A Corporation Not-for-Profit
ANNUAL MEMBERS MEETING MINUTES

The meeting was called to order at 7:30 p.m., Monday, January 15, 2015, in the Recreation Hall by the President. The President announced that the first order of business was the calling of the roll and the certifying of the proxies. Upon its completion, it was announced that one hundred (100) members were represented in person and fifty (50) members were represented by proxy. The President declared that a quorum of the two hundred (200) parcels was present.

The President next called upon the Secretary to present the affidavit for proof of notice and directed it to be annexed to the minutes of the meeting and made a permanent part of the Association's official records. The President stated that the next item of business was the reading of the minutes from the last members' meeting. Upon a motion made by Mr. Jones and seconded by Mr. Smith, and upon discussion, it was unanimously carried by voice vote that the reading of the minutes be waived.

The next item of business was the appointment of inspectors of election. The President appointed the Association's Vice President, Sara Harris, and Mr. Campbell to serve as inspectors of election and directed that all ballots be turned over to the inspectors for tabulation. The President then stated that, without objection, the meeting would stand in recess until the tabulation of the ballots was completed.

Upon reconvening the recessed meeting, the President called upon the Vice President to announce the results of the election. The Vice President then stated that the following individuals were elected to serve for a term of one year on the Board of Directors:
> Baylor Thomas
> Tyler Owen
> Conner Wesley

The next order of business was the reports of officers and committees. The President recognized the Treasurer who gave the financial report for the preceding twelve months. Upon completion of the presentation, the President directed that it be annexed to the minutes of the meeting and distributed to the membership.

Under report of committees, the President recognized the Chairman of the Recreation Committee, Mr. Johnson, who presented the schedule of functions and events planned for the coming calendar year.

The President next asked for items of unfinished business. There being no unfinished business, the President then stated that the next item on the agenda was consideration of new business. Mr. Wesley moved that amendments to the bylaws be adopted. The motion was seconded, and, at the conclusion of the discussion, the amendments were approved by a vote of 138 yeas and 12 nays.

There being no further new business to come before the meeting and no further member seeking recognition, upon a motion duly made, seconded, and unanimously carried, the President stated that the meeting was adjourned at the hour of 8:30 p.m.

_____
Secretary

BALLOT

1. The following have been nominated to serve for a term of one year on the Board of Directors of the Homeowners Association. There are three (3) vacancies on the Board of Directors and you may vote for up to three individuals by placing a check mark next to their names. A ballot voting for more than three individuals will be disallowed.

    Sara Harris   _____

    Baylor Thomas   _____

    William Marshall   _____

    Tyler Owen   _____

    Conner Wesley   _____

2. Should the Bylaws of Cypress Homeowners Association, Inc., be amended to allow for directors to serve for a term of two (2) years in accordance with the full text of the proposed amendment which accompanied the mailing of the meeting notice?

    Yes_____   No_____

Form 10.1-7 Ballot for Board Election

INSTRUCTIONS FOR COMPLETING
ELECTION BALLOT

Balloting for the board of directors is secret. Eligible members of the homeowners association are entitled to vote on the day of the election by returning the enclosed ballot to the Secretary of the Association. An association member wishing to vote by using the enclosed ballot shall comply with the following instructions:

1. Mark the ballot for the candidates of the voter's choice. Do not place any identifying marks such as the voter's name or unit number on the ballot.

2. Place the completed ballot in the plain ("inner") envelope enclosed and seal the envelope securely. A separate envelope must be used for each marked ballot, if eligible.

3. Place the sealed plain envelope containing the marked ballot in the second envelope addressed to the association Secretary and seal securely.

4. Sign the envelope and identify the unit that the voter represents adjacent to the eligible voter's signature.

5. Return the envelope to the Secretary of the Association prior to the time for tabulating the ballots.

CYPRESS HOMEOWNERS ASSOCIATION, INC.
A Corporation Not-for-Profit

ROSTER OF PARCEL OWNERS

PARCEL NUMBER	PARCEL OWNER	DESIGNATED VOTER
101	Sara Harris 101 Cypress Lane Cypress Springs, FL 33444 Tel. No. (111) 999-7101	Sara Harris
102	Matthew Marshall Amy Jo Marshall 102 Cypress Lane Cypress Springs, FL 33444 (no telephone)	Matthew Marshall
103	Peter Johnson Susan Johnson 103 Cypress Lane Cypress Springs, FL 33444 (telephone no. unknown)	Susan Johnson
104	David R. Smith Nancy H. Smith 104 Cypress Lane Cypress Springs, FL 33444 Tel. No. (111) 999-7104	David R. Smith
105	Marc Wesley Chollet Wesley 105 Cypress Lane Cypress Springs, FL 33444 Tel. No. (111) 999-7105	Marc Wesley

Form 10.1-9 Roster of Parcel Owners

106   ABP Corporation   Tyler Owen
                113 Main Street
                Cypress Springs, FL 33444
                Tel. No. (111) 999-7106
                Attn: Tyler Owen, Pres.

CYPRESS HOMEOWNERS ASSOCIATION, INC.
A Corporation Not-for-Profit

NOTICE OF MEETING

TO: Members of the Board of Directors

1. Sara Harris
2. Ann Lindsey
3. Tyler Owen
4. Conner Wesley
5. William Marshall

NOTICE IS HEREBY GIVEN that a meeting of the Board of Directors of Cypress Homeowners Association, Inc., will be held at the following date, time, and place:

Date: January 16, 2015

Time: 9:00 a.m.

Place: Recreation Hall
Cypress Homeowners Association, Inc.
100 Cypress Lane
Cypress Springs, Florida 33444

Dated: January 10, 2015

_____
Secretary

CYPRESS HOMEOWNERS ASSOCIATION, INC.
A Corporation Not-for-Profit

WAIVER OF NOTICE OF MEETING
OF BOARD OF DIRECTORS

We, the undersigned, being all of the members of the Board of Directors hereby agree and consent to the meeting of the Board to be held on the date and time, and at the place designated hereunder, and do hereby waive all notice whatsoever of such meeting and of any adjournment, or adjournments, thereof.

We do further agree and consent that any and all lawful business may be transacted at such meeting, or at any adjournment or adjournments thereof, as may be deemed advisable by the Board present thereat. Any business transacted at such meeting or at any adjournment or adjournments thereof, shall be as valid and legal and of the same force and effect as if such meeting, or adjourned meeting, were held after notice.

Place: Recreation Hall
           Cypress Homeowners Assn., Inc.
           100 Cypress Lane, Cypress Springs, FL 33444

Date: January 16, 2015

Time: 9:00 a.m.

Dated: January 10, 2015

_____   _____
Member, Board of Directors   Member, Board of Directors

_____   _____
Member, Board of Directors   Member, Board of Directors

Form 10.2-1 Waiver of Notice by Board Members

CYPRESS HOMEOWNERS ASSOCIATION, INC.
A Corporation Not-for-Profit

NOTICE TO ASSOCIATION MEMBERS OF
MEETING OF BOARD OF DIRECTORS

NOTICE IS HEREBY GIVEN that a meeting of the Board of Directors of Cypress Homeowners Association, Inc., will be held at the following date, time and place:

Place of Meeting: Recreation Hall
Cypress Homeowners Association, Inc.
100 Cypress Lane
Cypress Springs, Florida 33444

Date of Meeting: January 16, 2015

Time of Meeting: 9:00 a.m.

Agenda:

The order of business for the regular meeting of the Board of Directors shall be:

1. Reading of minutes of the previous meeting.

2. Comment and discussion by parcel owners.

3. Report of Manager.

4. Report of Officers.

5. Unfinished business.
   a) Matters relating to grounds and buildings.
   b) Matters relating to association financial affairs.

6. New business.

7. Adjournment.

Form 10.2-2 Notice of Board Meeting for Association Members

This notice has been posted upon the property this 13th day of January, 2015, by order of the Board of Directors and in compliance with §720.303 (2), F.S.

Dated:_____   _____
                       Secretary

CYPRESS HOMEOWNERS ASSOCIATION, INC.
A Corporation Not-for-Profit

PROOF OF NOTICE AFFIDAVIT

STATE OF FLORIDA
COUNTY OF PINELLAS

Comes now the undersigned Secretary of Cypress Homeowners Association, Inc., being first duly sworn, deposes and says that said Secretary has posted or caused to be posted, conspicuously on the property, and has mailed or delivered or caused to be mailed or delivered written notice of the meeting of the Board of Directors to be held on January 15, 2015, not less than seven (7) days prior to said meeting.

Dated this 5th day of January, 2015.

_____
Secretary

The foregoing Affidavit was acknowledged before me this 5th day of January, 2015, by Nancy Thomas, the Secretary of Cypress Homeowners Association, Inc.

_____
Notary Public

My commission expires:

CYPRESS HOMEOWNERS ASSOCIATION, INC.
A Corporation Not-for-Profit

AGENDA FOR REGULAR MEETING
OF THE BOARD OF DIRECTORS

The order of business for the regular meeting of the Board of Directors shall be as follows:

1. Reading of minutes of the previous meeting.

2. Comment and discussion by parcel owners on all matters to be considered by the Board.

3. Report of Manager.

4. Report of Officers.

5. Unfinished business.
   a) Matters relating to grounds and buildings.
   b) Matters relating to association financial affairs.

6. New business.
   a) Matters relating to contract bids.
   b) Scheduling of annual members meeting.

7. Adjournment.

Form 10.2-4 Agenda of Board Meeting

CYPRESS HOMEOWNERS ASSOCIATION, INC.
A Corporation Not-for-Profit

WRITTEN ACTION BY THE
BOARD OF DIRECTORS

The Board of Directors of Cypress Homeowners Association, Inc., determining that an emergency exists, and, by unanimous written action, adopts the following resolutions:

1. RESOLVED, that the windstorm damage caused to the roof of the Recreation Building be repaired immediately to prevent further damage to the interior of the building.

2. RESOLVED, that the President of the Association be and is hereby authorized and directed to obtain three bids and to accept the lowest responsible bid for the purpose of commencing the repairs to the roof of the Recreation Building.

3. RESOLVED, that sufficient monies be made available from the reserve fund for the roof for the purpose of paying for the repair to the Recreation Building.

4. RESOLVED, that a special meeting of the Board of Directors be called, after proper notice has been given and posted for the benefit of all the members, for the purpose of reviewing these written actions of the Board of Directors and for discussing further the wind damage to the association property.

DONE by unanimous written consent this ___ day of January, 2015.

_____   _____
Member, Board of Directors   Member, Board of Directors

_____   _____
Member, Board of Directors   Member, Board of Directors

_____
Member, Board of Directors

Form 10.2-5 Written Action by Board Members

CYPRESS HOMEOWNERS ASSOCIATION, INC.
A Corporation Not-for-Profit

MINUTES OF MEETING OF THE
BOARD OF DIRECTORS

The meeting of the Board of Directors was held on the date, time, and at the place set forth in the notice of meeting fixing such time and place, and attached to the minutes of this meeting. Notice of the meeting was posted on the bulletin board in the Clubhouse forty-eight (48) hours prior to the meeting.

There were present the following:
Baylor Thomas
Ann Lindsey
William Marshall
Sara Harris
Tyler Owen

being all the members of the Board of Directors.

After the meeting was called to order, a motion was made, seconded, and unanimously adopted waiving the reading of the minutes from the previous meeting. The President then declared that the floor was open for comment and discussion by any parcel owner on any subject that was to be considered by the Board or on any other subject concerning the homeowners association.

Mr. Wesley, 105 Cypress Lane, addressed the Board regarding safety in the swimming area. The President advised that the Board would review the matter in more detail. Mrs. Jones, 101 Cypress Lane, next addressed the Board on the speed of vehicles passing along the main entrance road to the community. The President directed that the manager notify the City and request that the roadway area be more closely patrolled.

At the conclusion of comments by parcel owners, the President called upon the property manager. The manager presented a report on the bids for insurance for the coming year and recommended that the lowest bid be accepted. Upon a motion duly made, seconded and unanimously carried, it was

RESOLVED, that the bid of the Florida Insurance Company, being the lowest bid, be accepted and that they be directed to provide the insurance for the association property for the next calendar year.

The President stated that there were no reports of officers and no unfinished business. The President then asked if there was any new business to come before the meeting. There being no new business, and upon a motion duly made, seconded, and unanimously carried, the President declared the same adjourned.

Dated: _____   _____
                                                Secretary

OFFICIAL RECORDS LIST

1.   Copy of the plans, specifications, permits, warranties, and other items provided by the developer at the time of transition.

2.   Recorded copy of Declaration of Covenants and Restrictions of the Homeowners Association and all amendments.

3.   Copy of the Articles of Incorporation of the Association and all amendments.

4.   Copy of the Association Bylaws and all amendments.

5.   Copy of all current Rules and Regulations, Policy Statements, and Resolutions of Procedure.

6.   Minutes for all meetings of the board of directors and of the membership for at least seven (7) years.

7.   Current roster of all parcel owners, their mailing addresses, voting certificates and, if known, telephone numbers.

8.   All current insurance policies for the Association.

9.   Management agreement, lease agreements, and other contracts under which the Association is responsible.

10.   Bills of sale, deeds to common property, easements, and other recorded documents.

11.   Financial and accounting records for the Association and separate accounting records for any fees and charges for recreational amenities. The accounting records shall be maintained for at least seven (7) years and shall include but are not limited to:

       a) Accurate, itemized, and detailed records of all receipts and expenditures;

Form 10.2-7 Official Records List

b) A current accounting for each parcel owner, with assessment amount, the amount paid, and the balance due;

c) All audits, reviews, accounting statements, and financial reports of the Association;

d) All contracts for work to be performed for the Association (bids shall also be considered official records and shall be kept for at least one year).

12. Budget and annual financial report provided to the Association membership.

13. All tax returns, financial statements, and financial reports of the Association.

14. All other records of the Association that identify, measure, record, or communicate financial information.

ACCEPTANCE OF APPOINTMENT OF REGISTERED AGENT AND DESIGNATION OF REGISTERED OFFICE

Pursuant to the provisions of Section 617.0501 and 617.0502, Florida Statutes, Cypress Homeowners Association, Inc., organized under the laws of the State of Florida, submits this statement for the purpose of changing its registered office and registered agent in the State of Florida as authorized by a resolution duly adopted by the Board of Directors on the 10th day of January, 2015, to the following:

BAYLOR THOMAS
101 Cypress Drive
Cypress Springs, Florida 33444

Date: _____   _____
                                                    Secretary

ACKNOWLEDGMENT

Having been named to accept service of process for the above stated corporation, at the place designated in this certificate, I hereby accept to act in this capacity, and agree to comply with the provisions of the law relative to keeping open said office.

Date: _____   _____
                                              Registered Agent

CYPRESS HOMEOWNERS ASSOCIATION, INC.
A Corporation Not-for-Profit

A RESOLUTION OF THE BOARD OF DIRECTORS CREATING A COMMITTEE OF THE BOARD TO SELECT AND RECOMMEND A MANAGER FOR THE HOMEOWNERS ASSOCIATION.

BE IT HEREBY RESOLVED by the Board of Directors of Cypress Homeowners Association, Inc., as follows:

Section 1. THAT a committee for the selection of a manager of the homeowners association is hereby created, and Joseph A. Jones, Nancy Thomas, and David Smith are appointed to serve as members of the committee. Nancy Thomas shall serve as the chairman of the committee.

Section 2. THAT the committee shall have the authority to expend up to $500.00 in costs for advertisements and other related expenses in recruiting potential candidates for the position of manager.

Section 3. THAT the committee shall have the authority to investigate and interview candidates on behalf of the Board of Directors and shall select from the candidates the three individuals which the committee feels are best qualified to fill the position of manager and shall recommend them, in order of preference, to the full Board of Directors prior to the next regular quarterly meeting.

Section 4. THAT the committee shall not be authorized to hire any individual for the position of manager or otherwise expend, or commit to expend, any funds of the Association except as specifically authorized by this resolution.

ADOPTED by the Board of Directors this 10th day of January, 2015.

CYPRESS HOMEOWNERS
ASSOCIATION, INC.

(CORPORATE SEAL)

By:_____
President

ATTEST:

_____
Secretary

CYPRESS HOMEOWNERS ASSOCIATION, INC.
A Corporation Not-for-Profit

DECLARATION OF THE PRESIDENT

COMES NOW, Peter Johnson, President of Cypress Homeowners Association, Inc., and does hereby exercise the authority granted in the bylaws of the Association and does state and declare as follows:

1.   THAT there is created a bylaw committee to study and evaluate the recent amendments to the law and to make a review of the bylaws of the Homeowners Association.

2.   THAT the membership for the committee shall consist of Matthew Marshall, Marc Wesley, and Sara Harris. Sara Harris is hereby designated to serve as chairman of the committee.

3.   THAT the committee shall make recommendations for proposed amendments to the bylaws which govern the Homeowners Association and shall advise the President on any amendments to the law which may require changes to the policies and procedures of the Association.

4.   THAT the committee shall not have the authority to act for or to bind the Homeowners Association nor shall it have the authority to expend any funds of the Association. The existence of the committee shall terminate upon submitting its final report to the President.

DONE this 30th day of September, 2015.

By:_____
     President

CYPRESS HOMEOWNERS ASSOCIATION, INC.
A Corporation Not-for-Profit

REPORT OF THE SPECIAL BYLAW COMMITTEE

TO: PRESIDENT AND MEMBERS OF THE
BOARD OF DIRECTORS, CYPRESS
HOMEOWNERS ASSOCIATION, INC.

FROM: SPECIAL BYLAW COMMITTEE, BY
APPOINTMENT OF THE PRESIDENT
SEPTEMBER 30, 2015

The special bylaw committee met on three occasions, after posting notice forty-eight (48) hours in advance of each meeting, to evaluate the amendments to the law and to consider amendments to the Association's bylaws. As a result of the committee's study, the following changes are recommended:

1. The Association establish a standing committee for budget and finance.

2. The Association revise its fining policy to limit the amount to no more than $100.00.

3. The Association establish a uniform procedure for reviewing new owners and providing them copies of the governing documents.

The committee additionally recommends the following changes and additions be made to the bylaws of the Association:

1. Addition of a section to provide for voluntary binding arbitration of disputes between owners and the Association.

2. Deletion of the section allowing members of the Board of Directors to abstain from voting.

3. Amendment to the section of the bylaws relating to the term of

Form 10.3-3 Committee Report

office for board members to permit members to serve for staggered terms of two years.

Respectfully submitted this 30th day of September, 2015.

_____
Chairman

_____
Member

_____
Member

CYPRESS HOMEOWNERS ASSOCIATION, INC.
A Corporation Not-for-Profit

2015 BUDGET

I. Expenses for the Association	Monthly	Annually
A. Administration of Association	$ 100.00	$ 1,200.00
B. Management Fees	702.00	8,424.00
C. Building Cleanup and Maintenance	100.00	1,200.00
D. Lawn and Property Maintenance	500.00	6,000.00
E. Rent for Recreation and Other Commonly Used Facilities	100.00	1,200.00
F. Expenses on Association Property		
1) Taxes	21.00	252.00
2) Cleaning and Maintenance	10.00	120.00
G. Taxes on Leased Property	10.00	120.00
H. Electricity	320.00	3,840.00
I. Water, Sewer, and Garbage Service	900.00	10,800.00
J. Insurance	625.00	7,500.00
K. Miscellaneous		
1) Publication Subscriptions	2.00	24.00
2) Professional Services (legal and accounting)	100.00	1,200.00
L. Pest Control	100.00	1,200.00
TOTAL	$ 3,590.00	$ 43,080.00

Form 10.4-0 Budget

II. Reserves

A. Building Painting	$ 384.00	$ 4,608.00
B. Pavement Resurfacing	75.00	900.00
C. Roof Replacement	250.00	3,000.00
D. Miscellaneous Reserves	50.00	00.00
TOTAL	$ 759.00	$ 9,108.00

1. The balance in the reserve accounts of the Association at the beginning of the current budget year was as follows:

a) Building painting	$ 23,040.00
b) Pavement resurfacing	$ 7,200.00
c) Roof replacement	$ 24,000.00
d) Miscellaneous reserves	$ 3,000.00

2. The formula for each reserve category is based on the following estimates:

a) Building painting to occur every eight (8) years and one-eighth of the total estimated cost is allocated to each fiscal year. Six of the eight years are currently on deposit.

b) Pavement resurfacing to occur every fifteen (15) years and one-fifteenth of the total estimated cost is allocated to each fiscal year. Nine of the fifteen years are currently on deposit.

c) Roof replacement to occur every twenty (20) years and one-twentieth of the total estimated cost is allocated to each fiscal year. Eight of the twenty years are currently on deposit.

d) Miscellaneous items of deferred maintenance and capital expenditures are based upon the needs for such expenditures as determined over the previous ten (10) years of the association and to cover needs not specifically identified in paragraphs (a), (b), and (c).

Form 10.4-0 Budget

CYPRESS HOMEOWNERS ASSOCIATION, INC.
A Corporation Not-for-Profit

2014 ANNUAL FINANCIAL REPORT

I. Expenses for the Association	Expenditures	
	Budgeted	**Actual**
A. Administration of Association	$ 1,200.00	$1,200.00
B. Management Fees	8,424.00	8,424.00
C. Building Cleaning and Maintenance	1,200.00	1,200.00
D. Lawn and Property Maintenance	6,000.00	5,750.00
E. Rent for Recreation and Other Commonly Used Facilities	1,200.00	1,200.00
F. Expenses on Association Property		
1) Taxes	252.00	252.00
2) Cleaning and Maintenance	120.00	250.00
G. Taxes on Leased Property	120.00	120.00
H. Electricity (common elements)	3,840.00	2,910.00
I. Water, Sewer, and Garbage Service	10,800.00	11,300.00
J. Insurance	7,500.00	7,489.00
K. Miscellaneous		
1) Publication Subscriptions	24.00	24.00
2) Professional Services (legal and accounting)	1,200.00	1,300.00
L. Pest Control	1,200.00	1,000.00
TOTAL	$ 43,080.00	$ 42,419.00

II. Income

A. Assessment Collection from Parcel Owners	$ 52,188.28
B. Interest Income from Operation Account	186.16
C. 2014 Surplus	210.12
TOTAL	$ 52,584.56

III. Summary

A. TOTAL INCOME	$ 52,584.56
B. TOTAL EXPENSES FOR OPERATIONS	-42,419.00
SUBTOTAL	$ 10,165.56
C. TOTAL RESERVE COLLECTIONS (2012)	-9,108.00
COMMON SURPLUS	$ 1,057.56

IV. Reserves

	Building Painting	Pavement Resurfacing	Roof Replacement	Misc Reserves
Beginning Balance	$ 16,996.00	$ 5,835.00	$ 25,200.00	$ 2,220.00
2014 Expenditures	4,608.00	900.00	3,000.00	600.00
Interest Earned	1,436.00	465.00	1,800.00	180.00
SUBTOTAL	$ 23,040.00	$ 7,200.00	$ 30,000.00	$ 3,000.00
2014 Expenditures	0.00	0.00	6,000.00	0.00
TOTAL RESERVES AT 2014 YEAR END	$ 23,040.00	$ 7,200.00	$ 24,000.00	$ 3,000.00

Form 10.4-1 Annual Financial Report

NOTICE OF INTENT TO RECORD A CLAIM OF LIEN
BY
CYPRESS HOMEOWNERS ASSOCIATION, INC.
A Corporation Not-for-Profit

RE: Parcel or (lot/block)…(lot/parcel number)… of Cypress Subdivision

The following amounts are currently due on your account to Cypress Homeowners Association, Inc., and must be paid with 45 days after your receipt of this letter. This letter shall serve as the association's notice of intent to record a Claim of Lien against your property no sooner than 45 days after your receipt of this letter, unless you pay in the full the amounts set forth below:

Maintenance due …(dates)…	$ _____
Late fee, if applicable	$ _____
Interest through …(dates)…*	$ _____
Certified mail charges	$ _____
Other costs	$ _____
TOTAL OUTSTANDING	$ _____

*Interest accrues at the rate of _____ per annum.

CLAIM OF LIEN
BY
CYPRESS HOMEOWNERS ASSOCIATION, INC.
A Corporation Not-for-Profit

STATE OF FLORIDA
COUNTY OF PINELLAS

In accordance with the authority of the Declaration of Covenants of Cypress Estates, CYPRESS HOMEOWNERS ASSOCIATION, INC., hereby claims a lien for all unpaid assessments now delinquent and hereafter accrued against the parcel and owner described below, in the initial amount and from the date stated, together with interest and reasonable attorney's fees and costs incident to the collection hereof, as follows:

Owner Due Date	Assessment	
Marc Wesley	June 15, 2014	$100.00

PROPERTY DESCRIPTION

Lot 5, CYPRESS ESTATES, according to the map or plat thereof recorded in Plat Book 8, Page 10, Public Records of Pinellas County, Florida.

EXECUTED this 15th day of September, 2014.

(CORPORATE SEAL)   CYPRESS HOMEOWNERS
                ASSOCIATION, INC.

ATTEST:

_____   By:_____
Secretary   President

    SWORN TO and subscribed before me this 15th day of September, 2014, by BAYLOR THOMAS, President, for the purpose therein expressed.

My commission expires: _____
                            Notary Public

    Personally Known ___ OR Produced _____ as identification.

CYPRESS HOMEOWNERS ASSOCIATION, INC.
100 Cypress Lane
Cypress, Florida 33444

July 20, 2015

Mr. Marc Wesley
105 Cypress Lane
Cypress, Florida 33444

Re: DELINQUENT ASSESSMENT (Claim of Lien, Unit 105, Waterfront XX Condominium)

Dear Mr. Wesley:

This letter is to inform you a Claim of Lien has been filed against your property because you have not paid the …(type of assessment)… assessment to Cypress Homeowners Association, Inc. The association intends to foreclose the lien and collect the unpaid amount within 30 days of this letter being sent to you.

You owe the interest accruing from …(month/year)… to the present. As of the date of this letter, the total amount due with interest is $ _____. All costs of any action and interest from this day forward will also be charged to your account.

Any questions concerning this matter should be directed to …(insert name, addresses, and telephone numbers of association representative)…

Cypress Homeowners Association, Inc.

_____

Form 10.4-4 Notice of Intent to Foreclose Lien

RELEASE OF LIEN
BY
CYPRESS HOMEOWNERS ASSOCIATION, INC.
A Corporation Not-for-Profit

The undersigned lienor, in consideration of the final payment in the amount of $_____, hereby waives and releases its lien and right to claim a lien for unpaid assessments through _____, recorded in Official Records Book 1000, Page 100, Public Records of Pinellas County, Florida, from the following described real property:

Lot 105, of Cypress Estates according to the map or plat thereof, recorded in Plat Book 109, Page, 10, of the Public Records of Pinellas County, Florida.

    DONE AND EXECUTED this 23rd day of October, 2015.

_____CYPRESS HOMEOWNERS
Witness: print name _____ ASSOCIATION, INC.

_____By: _____
Witness: print name _____Joseph A. Jones, President

    On this 23rd day of October, 2015, personally appeared, JOSEPH A. JONES, President, and acknowledged that he executed this Release of Lien for the purpose therein expressed.

        _____
        Notary Public

    My commission expires:

Personally Known ___ OR Produced _____ as identification.

DISCLOSURE SUMMARY
FOR
CYPRESS HOMEOWNERS ASSOCIATION, INC.

1. AS A PURCHASER OF PROPERTY IN THIS COMMUNITY, YOU WILL BE OBLIGATED TO BE A MEMBER OF A HOMEOWNERS ASSOCIATION.

2. THERE HAVE BEEN OR WILL BE RECORDED RESTRICTIVE COVENANTS GOVERNING THE USE AND OCCUPANCY OF PROPERTIES IN THIS COMMUNITY.

3. YOU WILL BE OBLIGATED TO PAY ASSESSMENTS TO THE ASSOCIATION. ASSESSMENTS MAY BE SUBJECT TO PERIODIC CHANGE. IF APPLICABLE, THE CURRENT AMOUNT IS $_____ PER _____. YOU WILL ALSO BE OBLIGATED TO PAY ANY SPECIAL ASSESSMENTS IMPOSED BY THE ASSOCIATION. SUCH SPECIAL ASSESSMENTS MAY BE SUBJECT TO CHANGE. IF APPLICABLE, THE CURRENT AMOUNT IS $_____ PER _____.

4. YOU MAY BE OBLIGATED TO PAY SPECIAL ASSESSMENTS TO THE RESPECTIVE MUNICIPALITY, COUNTY, OR SPECIAL DISTRICT. ALL ASSESSMENTS ARE SUBJECT TO PERIODIC CHANGE.

5. YOUR FAILURE TO PAY THESE SPECIAL ASSESSMENTS OR ASSESSMENTS LEVIED BY A MANDATORY HOMEOWNERS ASSOCIATION COULD RESULT IN A LIEN ON YOUR PROPERTY.

6. THERE MAY BE AN OBLIGATION TO PAY RENT OR LAND USE FEES FOR RECREATIONAL OR OTHER COMMONLY USED FACILITIES AS AN OBLIGATION OF MEMBERSHIP IN THE HOMEOWNERS ASSOCIATION. IF APPLICABLE, THE CURRENT AMOUNT IS $_____ PER _____.

7. THE DEVELOPER MAY HAVE THE RIGHT TO AMEND THE RESTRICTIVE COVENANTS WITHOUT THE APPROVAL OF THE ASSOCIATION MEMBERSHIP OR THE APPROVAL OF THE PARCEL OWNERS.

Form 10.5-0 Disclosure Summary

8. THE STATEMENTS CONTAINED IN THIS DISCLOSURE FORM ARE ONLY SUMMARY IN NATURE, AND, AS A PROSPECTIVE PURCHASER, YOU SHOULD REFER TO THE COVENANTS AND THE ASSOCIATION GOVERNING DOCUMENTS BEFORE PURCHASING PROPERTY.

9. THESE DOCUMENTS ARE EITHER MATTERS OF PUBLIC RECORD AND CAN BE OBTAINED FROM THE RECORD OFFICE IN THE COUNTY WHERE THE PROPERTY IS LOCATED, OR ARE NOT RECORDED AND CAN BE OBTAINED FROM THE DEVELOPER.

DATE:_____   _____
                            PURCHASER

                            _____
                            PURCHASER

Table of Cases

Abbey Properties Co., Inc. v. Presidential Insurance Co., 119 So.2d 74 (Fla. 2d DCA 1960).

Aquarian Foundation, Inc. v. Sholom House, Inc., 448 So.2d 1166, 1168 (Fla. 3d DCA 1984).

Acquisition Corp. v. Markborough Prop., 568 So.2d 1350 (Fla. 4th DCA 1990).

Acopian v. Halley, 387 So.2d 392 (Fla. 5th DCA 1980), *rev. den.*, 392 So.2d 1375 (Fla. 1981).

Advisory Opinion of the Florida Attorney General, AGO 99-53.

Advisory Opinion of the Florida Attorney General, AGO 01-01.

Andres v. Indian Creek Phase III-B Homeowner's Ass'n, 901 So.2d 182 (Fla. 4th DCA 2005).

Ass'n of Poinciana v. Avatar Properties, 724 So.2d 585 (Fla. 5th DCA 1998).

B & J Holding Corp. v. Weiss, 353 So.2d 141 (Fla. 3d DCA 1977).

BHB Development v. Bonefish Yacht Club Homeowners Ass'n, 691 So.2d 1174 (Fla. 3d DCA 1997).

Backus v. Smith, 363 So.2d 786 (Fla. 1st DCA 1978).

Balzer v. Indian Lake Maintenance, Inc., 346 So.2d 146 (Fla. 3d DCA 1977).

Barrwood Homeowners Ass'n, Inc. v. Maser, 675 So.2d 983 (Fla. 4th DCA 1996).

Barton v. Moline Properties, 121 Fla. 683, 164 So. 551 (Fla. 1935).

Coral Lakes Community Ass'n, Inc. v. Busey Bank, 30 So.3d 579, 584 (Fla. 2d DCA 2010).

Coleman v. Plantation Golf Club, Inc., 212 So.2d 806 (Fla. 4th DCA 1968).

Crissman v. Dedakis, 330 So.2d 103 (Fla. 1st DCA 1976).

Cudjoe Gardens Property Owners Ass'n v. Payne, 770 So.2d 190 (Fla. 3d DCA 2000).

Cudjoe Gardens Property Owners Ass'n v. Payne, 779 So.2d 598 (Fla. 3d DCA 2001).

Dade County Dairies, Inc. v. Projected Planning Co., 158 So.2d 565 (Fla. 3d DCA 1963).

Daniel v. May, 143 So.2d 536 (Fla. 3d DCA 1962).

David v. B & J Holding Corp., 349 So.2d 676 (Fla. 3d DCA 1977).

Demaio v. Coco Wood Lakes Ass'n, Inc., 637 So.2d 369 (Fla. 4th DCA 1994).

Don Cesar Property Owners Corp. v. Gallagher, 452 So.2d 1047 (Fla. 2d DCA 1984).

Dornbach v. Holley, 854 So.2d 211 (Fla. 2d DCA 2002).

Eastpointe Prop. Owners' Ass'n v. Cohen, 505 So.2d 518 (Fla. 4th DCA 1987).

Eberwein v. Coral Pine Condominium One, 431 So.2d 616 (Fla. 4th DCA 1983).

Ecoventure WGV, Ltd. V. Saint Johns Northwest Residential Ass'n, Inc., 56 So.3d 126 (Fla. 5th DCA 2011).

Edward J. Gerrits, Inc. v. McKinney, 410 So.2d 542 (Fla. 1st DCA 1982).

Emerald Estates Community Assoc., Inc. v. Gorodetzer, 819 So.2d 190 (Fla. 4th DCA 2002).

Golian v. Polhironakis, 390 So.2d 187 (Fla. 2d DCA 1980).

Hagan v. Sabal Palms, Inc., 186 So.2d 302 (Fla. 2d DCA 1966).

Harris v. Sunset Island Property Owners, 116 So.2d 622 (Fla. 1958).

Harwick v. Indian Creek Country Club, 142 So.2d 128 (Fla. 3d DCA 1962).

Hawn v. Shoreline Towers Phase I Condominium Ass'n, Inc., 347 Fed Appx. 464 (N.D. Fla. 2009).

Heath v. Bear Island Homeowners Ass'n, Inc., 76 So.3d 39 (Fla. 4th DCA 2011).

Heck v. Parkview Place Homeowners Ass'n, Inc., 642 So.2d 1201 (Fla. 4th DCA 1994).

Heron at Destin West Beach and Bay Resort Condominium Ass'n, Inc. v. Osprey at Destin West and Bay Resort Condominium Ass'n, Inc., 94 So.2d 623 (Fla. 1st DCA 2012).

Hidden Harbour Estates v. Basso, 393 So.2d 637 (Fla. 4th DCA 1981).

Highland Lakes Prop. Owners v. Schlack, 724 So.2d 621 (Fla. 5th DCA 1998).

Holiday Pines v. Wetherington, 557 So.2d 243 (Fla. 4th DCA 1990).

Holiday Pines Prop. Owners v. Wetherington, 596 So.2d 84 (Fla. 4th DCA 1992).

Holly Lakes Ass'n v. Federal Nat. Mortg. Ass'n, 660 So.2d 266 (Fla. 1995).

Homeowner's Ass'n of Overlook, Inc. v. Seabrooke Homeowner's Ass'n, Inc., 62 So.3d 667 (Fla. 4th DCA 2011).

Ideal Foods, Inc. v. Action Leasing Corp., 413 So.2d 416 (Fla. 5th DCA 1982).

Imperial Golf Club, Inc. v. Monaco, 752 So.2d 653 (Fla. 2d DCA 2000).

Lakes of Emerald Hills v. Silverman, 558 So.2d 442 (Fla. 4th DCA 1990).

Lakeridge Greens Homeowners Assoc., Inc. v. Silberman, 765 So.2d 95 (Fla. 4th DCA 2000).

Lakewood on the Green Villas v. Pomerantz, 556 So.2d 505 (Fla. 4th DCA 1990).

Lancaster v. Banks, 492 So.2d 464 (Fla. 5th DCA 1986).

Latera v. Isle at Mission Bay Homeowners Ass'n, Inc., 655 So.2d 144 (Fla. 4th DCA 1995).

Lathan v. Hanover Woods Homeowners' Ass'n, 547 So.2d 319 (Fla. 5th DCA 1989).

Laursen v. Giolli, 549 So.2d 1174 (Fla. 2d DCA 1989).

Lensa Corp. v. Poinciana Gardens Ass'n, Inc., 765 So.2d 296 (Fla. 4th DCA 2000).

Lewis v. S & T Anchorage, Inc., 616 So.2d 478 (Fla. 3d DCA 1993).

Loch Haven Homeowners' Ass'n v. Nelle, 389 So.2d 697 (Fla. 2d DCA 1980).

Loch Ness Homeowners Ass'n, Inc. v. Pelaez, 730 So.2d 380 (Fla. 3d DCA 1999).

Lunohah Investments, LLC v. Gaskel, ___ So.3d ___, (Fla. 5th DCA 2013), 39 Fla. L. Weekly D41 (Fla. 5th DCA 2013)

Mayes v. Hale, 82 Fla. 35, 89 So. 364 (Fla. 1921).

McMillan v. The Oaks of Spring Hill Homeowners' Ass'n, 754 So.2d 160 (Fla. 5th DCA 2000).

Metro-Dade Investments, Co. v. Granada Lakes Villas Condominium, Inc., 74 So.3d 593 (Fla. 2d DCA 2011).

Parton v. Palomino Lakes Property Owners Ass'n, Inc., 928 So.2d 449 (Fla. 2d DCA 2006)

Pelican Bay Homeowners Ass'n, Inc. v. Sedita, 724 So.2d 684 (Fla. 5th DCA 1999).

Pelican Island Property Owners v. Murphy, 554 So.2d 1179 (Fla. 2d DCA 1989).

Pomerantz v. Woodlands Section 8 Association, 479 So.2d 794 (Fla. 4th DCA 1986).

Port Sewall Harbor & Tennis Club Owners Ass'n v. First Fed. Sav. & Loan, 463 So.2d 530 (Fla. 4th DCA 1985).

Powell v. Shumann Investments, Inc., 492 So.2d 850 (Fla. 1st DCA 1986).

Princeton Homes, Inc. v. Morgan, 38 So.3d 207 (Fla. 4th DCA 2010).

Prindable v. Ass'n of Apartment Owners of 2987 Kalakava, 304 F. Supp. 2d 1245 (D. Hawaii 2003).

Putnam v. Roudebush, 352 So.2d 908 (Fla. 2nd DCA 1977).

Quail Creek Property Owners Ass'n v. Hunter, 538 So.2d 1288 (Fla. 2d DCA 1989).

Regency Highlands Associates v. Sherwood, 388 So.2d 271 (Fla. 4th DCA 1980).

Rocek v. Markowitz, 492 So.2d 460 (Fla. 5th DCA 1986).

Rolling Oaks Homeowners' Ass'n v. Dade County, 492 So.2d 686 (Fla. 3d DCA 1986).

Romero v. Shadywood Villas Homeowners Ass'n, Inc., 657 So.2d 1193 (Fla. 3d DCA 1995).

Rosenberg v. Metrowest Master Ass'n, Inc., 116 So3d 641 (Fla. 5th DCA 2013).

Strathmore Gate-East at Lake St. George Homeowners' Ass'n v. Levitt Homes, 537 So.2d 657 (Fla. 2d DCA 1989).

Taco Bell of California v. Zappone, 324 So.2d 121 (Fla. 2d DCA 1975).

Tahiti Beach Homeowners Ass'n v. Pfeffer, 52 So.3d 808 (Fla. 3d DCA 2011).

Taylor Creek Village Ass'n v. Houghton, 349 So.2d 1219 (Fla. 3d DCA 1977).

Tempel v. Southern Homes of Palm Beach, LLC, 90 So.3d 848 (Fla. 3d DCA 2012).

Thomas v. Vision I Homeowners Ass'n, 981 So.2d 1 (Fla. 4th DCA 2007).

Thomkin Corp. v. Miller, 24 So.2d 48 (Fla. 1945).

Tri Par Land Develop. Corp. v. Henthorn, 241 So.2d 429 (Fla. 2d DCA 1970).

Vantage View, Inc. v. Bali East Development Corp., 421 So.2d 728 (Fla. 4th DCA 1982).

Velickovich v. Ricci, 391 So.2d 258 (Fla. 4th DCA 1980).

Venetian Isles Homeowners Assoc., Inc. v. Albrecht, 823 So.2d 813 (Fla. 2d DCA 2002).

Vetzel v. Brown, 86 So.2d 138 (Fla. 1956).

Villages at Mango Key v. Hunter Development, Inc., 763 So.2d 476 (Fla. 5th DCA 2000).

Voight v. Harbour Heights Improvement Ass'n, 218 So.2d 803 (Fla. 4th DCA 1969).

Webster v. Ocean Reef Community Ass'n, Inc., 994 So.2d 367 (Fla. 3rd DCA 2008).

Wenger v. Breakwater Homeowners' Ass'n, 423 So.2d 619 (Fla. 4th DCA 1982).

Index

C

Cable television, 8.4

Canasta, 7.14

Candidate for board of directors, 2.10, 2.11

Candidate for public office, 6.2

Capital expenses, 5.3–5.4

Capricious enforcement, 7.6

Carports, 8.2

Cash receipts and expenditures, 5.12

Certification, board, 3.2

Certified mail, 3.3, 3.5, 7.4

Certified recall, 3.5

Chairman, meeting, 2.6–2.9, 2.12, 3.8, 4.3

Charges, association, 1.5, 5.1

Charter, corporate, 1.7

Chief executive, 4.3, 4.6

Children, 7.7

Circuit Court, 3.3, 7.5, 9.9

City ordinances, 1.1

Civil Rights Act, 7.7

Classes of owners, 5.7

Clean Indoor Air Act, Florida, 2.16

Closed
  Circuit television, 3.10
  Meetings, 3.10

Clotheslines, 8.3

Code, building, 7.3, 8.8

Collection, assessments, 5.10

Commercial property, 1.1

Commercial venture, 7.7

Commingling funds, 5.3, 9.3

Committee, architectural, 3.12, 8.6, 8.7

Committees, 3.12, 4.3, 5.10, 7.5, 7.11

Common areas, 1.3, 2.16, 6.2, 6.9

Community

Concept, 1.1, 1.3, 6.1, 6.8, 7.1

Construction defects, 9.8, 9.9

Directory, 1.12

Manager, 1.13, 5.14

Memberships, 6.9

Property, 1.3, 6.2

Compensation, director, 3.1, 4.11

Competitive bidding, 5.14

Compiled financial statements, 5.12

Concrete walls, 8.2

Condominium, 1.1

Condominium Act, 1.1

Conference call meeting, 3.8

Confidential communications, 7.4

Confidential records, 6.6

Conflict of interest, 5.14

Congregate living facility, 7.7

Consent, written, 1.12, 3.5, 3.8

Consent voting, 2.9

Consistency of the documents, 1.10

Construction defects, 8.2, 9.8–9.9

Consumer price index, 6.9

Contract
  Competitive bidding, 5.14
  For sale, 1.6
  For services, 5.14
  Rights, 1.2, 1.6, 7.2
  Written, 5.14

Contracts, 5.14

Control of board, 9.6–9.7

Cooperative Act, 1.1

Copy machine, 6.6

Copies of documents, 6.6, 9.6

Corporate charter, 1.7

Corporate report, 5.13

Corporation not for profit, 1.7, 3.7

Corporations, Division of, 1.7, 4.7, 5.13

Costs, of collection, 5.8, 5.9

Council, executive, 3.12

Here are some other books from Pineapple Press on related topics. For a complete catalog, write to Pineapple Press, P.O. Box 3889, Sarasota, Florida 34230-3889, or call (800) 746-3275. Or visit our website at www.pineapplepress.com.

Condominium Concept, 14th Edition by Peter M. Dunbar. Written in clear, concise language, this is an indispensable working tool for officers, directors, homeowners, managers, realtors, and attorneys. Completely updated to reflect the latest Florida Statutes, this comprehensive volume includes 70 sample forms you can use as well as a complete subject index.

Resident-Owned Community Guide for Florida Cooperatives, 3rd Edition by Peter M. Dunbar and Ashley E. Gault. This is the first practical guide for operating cooperatives, including condominiums, timeshares, and mobile home communities. Completely cross-referenced to the latest Florida Statutes, this comprehensive volume includes 60 sample forms you can use as well as a complete subject index.

The Homeowners Association Manual, 5th Edition by Peter M. Dunbar and Marc W. Dunbar. This manual provides a step-by-step explanation of the requirements for meetings, membership voting, and the necessary parliamentary procedures. In addition to the comprehensive text, there are 28 forms and sample documents—all you need to run an effective homeowners association.

Florida Law: A Layman's Guide, 5th Edition by Gerald Keane. This practical guide is for anyone who needs to know the basics of Florida law. Covers property, family, business, and criminal law.

Florida Divorce Handbook, 6th Edition by Gerald Keane. Reflects the most recent changes in family law in Florida. It offers an overview of the divorce process, introduces the basic vocabulary and legal concepts associated with divorce, and familiarizes you with what to expect if you are planning to divorce in Florida or if you are already divorced and have questions about your rights.

Everglades Lawmen by James T. Huffstodt. From the first game wardens in the Everglades to present-day wildlife officers, law enforcement in the wild, untamed Everglades has kept pace with changing times. Meet the people who have dedicated their lives to protecting the wildlife and natural resources in the only Everglades on earth.